The Challenge of BEA

The Challenge of BEA

The story of a great airline's first 25 years

by Garry May

WOLFE PUBLISHING LTD   10 Earlham Street London WC2

ISBN 72340447 X

© Garry May, 1971

© Wolfe Publishing Ltd, 1971

MADE AND PRINTED IN GREAT BRITAIN BY
OXLEY PRESS LIMITED, LONDON AND EDINBURGH

CONTENTS

Were those the days ? Northolt Airport in 1949, with baggage being unloaded from a BEA DC-3

CHAPTER 1

FIRST BASE

THURSDAY 1ST AUGUST 1946 was a warm, close day in London and it looked as if it might rain. It was the eve of the Bank Holiday week-end. The London, Midland and Scottish railway company announced it would run 1,043 extra trains, the London and North Eastern Railway an extra 800 and the Great Western Railway 150. The Royal Society for the Prevention of Accidents appealed to holidaymakers: 'Obey warning signs, watch for ammunition dumps, don't bathe in places marked dangerous.'

Bobby Howes and Jack Hulbert were starring in 'Here Come the Boys' at the Saville Theatre in London's West End, Angela Baddeley and Emlyn Williams in 'The Winslow Boy' at the Lyric. Lionel Barrymore was featured in 'Three Wise Fools' at the Empire cinema, Leicester Square. Lights were going up all around London.

De Havilland shares slipped 3d to 43s 6d, Handley Page rose 1½d to 25s 4½d and Fairey by the same amount to 18s 7½d. The Ministry of Supply said next week at Newbury racecourse there would be a large sale of jeeps, plus 380 other vehicles acquired from dumps abandoned by the United States Army. Sydney Wooderson said he would run the mile for Blackheath Harriers at Catford Bridge sports ground the following evening. Len Hutton said nothing and made 171 not out for Yorkshire against Northants at Hull.

The Prime Minister Mr Clement Atlee returned from a conference in Paris. His plane landed at Northolt, an aerodrome some 16 miles west of London which had been used by the Royal Air Force during the war. No-one seemed to notice that this was the day British European Airways was born or that Northolt was its birthplace.

The Civil Aviation Act, 1946, set up the airline, 'with a view to providing civil air services in various parts of the world and in particular in Europe (including the British Islands)'. But there were no fine words on this day, only a job of work to be done.

BEA was already in business and had been since 4th February when it was still a division of the British Overseas Airways Corporation. On that day it took over routes from No. 110 Wing, R.A.F. Transport Command and by starting up with a couple of new ones was at once flying to Amsterdam, Brussels, Helsinki, Lisbon, Madrid, Paris and Stockholm. All this was achieved with a handful of DC-3 Dakotas still in wartime camouflage and an energetic group of pilots who wore their old R.A.F. uniforms because they had nothing else. Markings and uniforms soon changed, but some of the war's ingrained flying habits led crews to exclaim that the pilots *must* remember they were not flying Spitfires any longer.

The number of Dakotas had risen to 21 by 1st August.

8   *Aerial view of Northolt Airport*

Many of the planes had already taken off from Northolt on early morning scheduled flights by the time new members of the staff had found their way to the airline's headquarters for their first day's work.

BEA's first base was, and still is, a complex of school buildings on the eastern perimeter of Northolt airport. Bourne Junior School was one of the 'new look' approaches to education with light, airy classrooms, gay pastel paintwork and central heating, opened on the eve of war in September 1939. But four days after the first pupils arrived they were called into the assembly hall (now a staff canteen) and told they were being moved out because the school was too close to the airfield's approaches. The school stood silent as Northolt became a Battle of Britain fighter station. When BEA moved in seven years later, it was like first day back at school all over again with chaos the lesson of the day.

The airline's first chairman was Sir Harold Hartley. He had Mr Whitney Straight as his deputy and Mr Gerard d'Erlanger as managing director. (*See Chapter* 9.) One of their first decisions was the adoption of the flying key, a symbol which they hoped would unlock the door to Europe. Bourne School became 'Keyline House' and soon afterwards the winged key was being painted across the tail fins of BEA's planes.

New routes to Prague and Rome had been added to the network within the first month. The start of a new service was almost a daily occurrence but 1st September brought one of significance. Out on to the tarmac rolled Valerie, one of the first of 75 Viking aircraft to be bought by BEA. The plane's design was based on the Wellington bomber, but with such a fat fuselage it quickly earned the nickname 'Pregnant Dakota'.

Being a Viking, it was only natural that Valerie should want to lead BEA into Europe via Scandinavia. So on 1st September 1946 Viking G–AHOP left Northolt for Copenhagen, the airline's first scheduled service to Europe with a British aircraft. Patriots said this was the *real*

beginning. The other dates were dismissed as false starts.

A fondness for naming individual aircraft persisted in BEA until the sixties. But even those passengers with the broadest senses of humour were staggered to find Valerie had as sisters Vagrant, Vagabond, Vampire, Varlet, Vandal, Villain, Vixen, Volatile and Vortex.

More and more new routes felt their way out of London to major cities in Europe like sensitive tentacles. Most of them took a firm hold, but while the new links were to be permanent there were still many temporary practices in operation. Pilots landing at Northolt blinked when they found taxiing instructions being flashed to them by Aldis lamp. Five department heads found themselves couped together in one small classroom with one typist while builders applied the finishing touches to extensions at the overcrowded school. New planes would arrive 'unfurnished' with no seats inside and some still had R.A.F. roundels on them.

But some of the amateur touches were a delight. Relatives could sit sipping afternoon tea at tables and chairs on the circle of grass in front of the terminal buildings. This was Northolt's waving base and visitors could await arrivals or smile their goodbyes only a few feet from where the matronly planes were rumbling by.

There was no hurry. Arriving passengers had to be checked by ticket collectors, medical officers, immigration officials, C.I.D. officers and customs men before boarding the coach to London.

Sometimes there was no-one to greet the arrivals. Many relatives who made their own way to Northolt for a re-union with heroes home from the war or fathers back from business trips, learned hours too late that half the airport was in Ruislip, the other half in Uxbridge and not one square inch in Northolt itself. As if to illustrate the point, one captain taxiing in from Paris, halted his aircraft alongside the spectators' enclosure where scores of schoolboys were watching. Opening a cockpit window he shouted:

Count E. Reventlow, with Mr. Gerard d'Erlanger, then BEA's managing director, christening the Viking Valerie on its first flight to Copenhagen in September, 1946

'Is this Northolt?'

'Yes,' laughed the delighted chorus.

'Oh, good,' said the captain, 'I've aimed straight at last!'

The Vikings were the pride of BEA's fleet, so it came as a shock when they were grounded in December 1946 because of engines and wings icing up in flight. They did not get a clean bill of health until the following April, but the airline in the meantime was doubling its operation. In assuming the second of the roles outlined by Parliament, BEA took over the services, staff and aircraft of the Associated Airways Joint Committee on 1st February 1947. At the same time it swallowed four companies no longer operating, then in April absorbed two others. This was the start of the corporation's domestic services.

The ten airlines taken over were:

Allied Airways (Gandar Dower)
Channel Islands Airways
Great Western & Southern Airlines
Highland Airways
Isle of Man Air Services
North Eastern Airways
Railway Air Services
West Coast Air Services
Scottish Airways
Western Isles Airways

Nationalisation suited the government of the day, but supporters of private enterprise and the airlines themselves fought bitterly against the take-overs. Some of the sting from the blow to Railway Air Services was soothed by the disappearance at the same time of the railway companies as privately owned concerns.

Surveying their newly-won trophies, BEA discovered they now had a motley collection of aircraft, few spares and some reluctant pilots. They had acquired two DC-3 Dakotas, eight Junkers Ju 52/3ms, 13 Avro 19s and a grand total of 45 de Havilland DH89 Dragon Rapide biplanes. The Junkers had come from Germany as war reparations. They had an ugly third engine on their noses and corrugated metal fuselages. BEA named the Junkers 'Jupiters' and adopted the R.A.F. name 'Dominie' for the Rapides. The new names neither helped the plight of the German aircraft nor affected the reputation of the biplane. Within twelve months the Jupiters along with the Avro 19s had been abandoned. Replacements for the Rapides were sought in 1948, but some of them stayed in BEA's colours until 1964.

The official reason for splitting off the new airline had been that the work it undertook was so different from that being done by BOAC. Now reasons had to be found for gobbling up the independent operators, some of whom had started as long ago as 1933. BEA got its monopoly on domestic routes because ruinous competition had to be avoided, the argument went. Later on, all this was conveniently forgotten when newly formed independents were granted routes parallel to those of the corporation.

While competition at home was crushed, BEA was fostering associated companies which in time were to become its rivals in Europe. They were Aer Lingus and Alitalia, now the national airlines of Ireland and Italy. BEA had a 30 per cent holding in Aer Lingus and a 40 per cent share of Alitalia.

Taking stock of their position in March 1947, the board of directors found that BEA had flown 58,618 passengers on international flights in eight months and 12,559 on journeys within Britain in two months. The 5,731 employees were staggered to learn that a loss of £2,157,937 had been incurred at the end of the first financial year. It represented £30 per passenger!

The fleet consisted of 22 Dakotas, 11 Jupiters, 29 Vikings, 45 Rapides and 12 Avro 19s. In addition, there were seven communications aircraft—two Austers, an Anson, Avro 19, M.28 Mercury, Gipsy Moth and a Rapide. By the time the first annual report had been published, Sir Harold Hartley and Mr Whitney Straight had resigned from the board and gone over to BOAC. The new chairman was Mr d'Erlanger, who had been managing director. Mr John Keeling became his deputy.

The first set of figures also included 510 tons of mail carried and 668 tons of freight. Loaders found that 'freight' could mean anything. Before long BEA's cargo planes had carried a couple of deer for the Duke of Bedford's estate, a privately owned herd of one bull, 24 cows and six heifers, and a tortoise which objected to heights over 10,000 feet on the way back from Turkey.

Onlookers at Northolt were sometimes allowed to eavesdrop and learn something of the glamorous world of flying. They could listen to conversations between aircraft crews and ground control when exchanges on some of the departing and arriving flights were relayed through the airport's public address system. The idea was to instil confidence by letting people hear how calm the pilots and

Badges of the Rail-Sea group of air companies incorporated in BEA in 1947

controllers were. One day a Viking happened to pass the new offices being erected at the west end of Northolt's administration block. The plane's slipstream caught an unsupported piece of framework and blew it flat. The manner in which the matter was discussed led to the broadcasting system being hurriedly switched off.

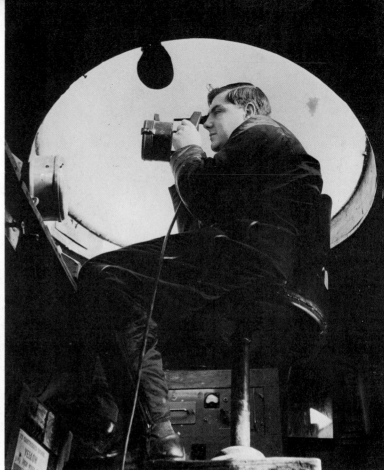

The control room at Northolt Airport, 1948

In 1947, the runway controller used an Aldis lamp to signal to aircraft on the ground

On another occasion a Viking was about to land at Northolt on a flight from Brussels. A leak in the hydraulic system of the undercarriage had caused the oil to drain away. The captain reviewed the choices—a belly landing, taking a chance on the wheels without hydraulic fluid, or somehow replacing the missing oil. He decided on the third course and called for all the tea and coffee left on board. The co-pilot flipped off the filler cap and the thick brown mixture was poured into the reservoir. It was not enough. The steward was sent back to his galley. He returned with the last stock of liquid on the plane—eight cans of lager beer. They brought the hideous cocktail frothing over the top and minutes later the aircraft made a perfect landing.

This was followed by one of the most extraordinary excursions ever undertaken by the airline. And it came at a time when BEA was still striving for confidence, recognition and self-respect. A Viking named 'Vitality' took off from Northolt at 11.17 a.m. bound for Paris. There were 25 passengers including Mr A. C. M. Spearman, Tory MP

Right: general view of Northolt control tower in 1948. Note staff transport in the foreground!

for Scarborough. At 12.47 on the dull December day the Viking reached Le Bourget airport on the outskirts of Paris, but thick fog prevented a landing. The pilot circled for half an hour without any sign of the fog lifting. The nearest landing field with clear visibility was Abbeville, 90 miles away, so the pilot headed for it.

He brought the plane down safely. But there was no-one to greet the plane and nothing in sight which remotely resembled a petrol pump. In the pilot's own words, 'It was just a main road.' So he took off again and headed back to Northolt. Strong cross winds were making landings tricky at Northolt and he was advised to divert to Heathrow, which he did. So in just over $4\frac{3}{4}$ hours the 25 passengers had been transported a distance of a few miles, having actually landed in France before returning. The MP immediately telephoned the Minister of Civil Aviation while the other passengers demanded an explanation from the airline.

Why come all the way back instead of waiting to go on to Paris? The plane might have run out of fuel in circling Le Bourget again, said an official. Why not wait at Abbeville until the fog cleared? There were no facilities to accommodate passengers. Why not put them on a train as Abbeville is on the main Calais–Paris line? There are no customs at Abbeville and it would have been illegal to put them on a train. And then to soften the blow, the spokesman added:

'But we are not altogether satisfied with the incident.'

One of the passengers scoffed, 'This is a good illustration of BEA's advertisement "BEA takes you there and brings you back." The trouble is they don't let you do anything in between.'

The following day, two Frenchmen who had been among the 25 were amazed to find they had a Viking all to themselves for their flight to Paris. The other 23 passengers, including Mr Spearman, had cancelled their bookings. Wearily, a BEA spokesman commented: 'If we had known we could have accommodated these two on a normal

Immigration control, 1947 vintage.
Below: a cup of tea in the Northolt buffet, 1947

service instead of laying on a special plane. The late cancellations have cost the taxpayers £200.'

Today's modern jets can fly at 600 mph. Even the most far-flung destinations on the airline's network are within six hours' flying time. But journeys lasting more than 24 hours were common in the Viking's day, even when everything went according to plan. Overnight stops were necessary on longer routes so that crews and passengers could catch up on their sleep. Regulations forbade pilots to fly more than a set number of hours without a break.

These were the travelling times from London taken by BEA aircraft in 1947:

Destination	Flights per week	Travelling time hours/mins.
Amsterdam	8	1–20
Ankara	1	28–30
Athens	3	11–05
Berlin	6	4–45
Bordeaux	10	2–40
Brussels	14	1–20
Copenhagen	4	3–20
Deauville	8	1–10
Frankfurt	3	2–30
Geneva	7	2–35
Gibraltar	2	7–55
Gothenburg	3	3–25
Hamburg	6	2–55
Helsinki	1	27–30
Istanbul	1	26–30
Lisbon	6	7–00
Madrid	4	5–05
Marseilles	4	3–20
Oslo	3	5–00
Paris	28	1–30
Prague	4	3–30
Rome	5	6–30
Stavanger	3	3–00
Stockholm	4	5–25
Vienna	3	6–00

Services to Ankara and Istanbul included a 13-hour night stop in Athens, and Helsinki passengers spent 15 hours overnight in Stockholm.

Many passengers saw for the first time the effects of six years of war. They had a bird's eye view of the major cities of Europe and of the devastation which had bombed-out vast areas in and around the historic capitals. But there were signs that the wounds were healing over with new buildings rising up and trees and plants masking scars in the countryside. For the flying crews, there was the joy of being safe in the air and of actually landing at places which had been targets on a bombing map less than three years before.

At home, BEA was packing up its belongings at Croydon airport and moving what remained of the staff to Northolt. The last scheduled service from Croydon was by Dragon

Weighing in – at 21 lbs – in Northolt Traffic Hall, 1950

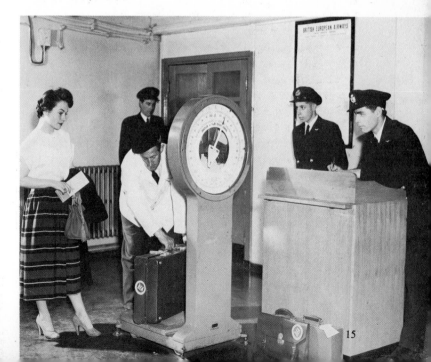

Rapide to the Channel Islands on 1st November 1947. Four months later, BEA had passed a total of half a million passengers for a year.

As if to celebrate, the board placed an order for 20 Airspeed Ambassadors. It was a surprise announcement and it baffled employees thrown out of work by the pruning of ten domestic services from the network. Destinations which suffered included Isle of Man, Carlisle, Cardiff, Belfast, Prestwick and Bristol. Most of them were still linked with main points on the network but it was no longer possible, for example, to fly from Belfast to Prestwick.

The services were withdrawn because they were totally uneconomic and there was no hope of improvement, said BEA. But the same might have been said of the cobweb of routes in Scotland which could have been brushed away with very little effort.

Even with its own headquarters, BEA was still leaning heavily on BOAC. Its London office was six rooms in BOAC's home at Berkeley Square. Changes took time. The battle to capture Bourne School had been fought right up to the Lord President of the Council. Winning the right from the R.A.F. to use the second half of a hangar at Northolt had taken four months. But by the summer of 1948 the fledgling had flown from BOAC's nest. Dorland Hall in Lower Regent Street was rented and passenger handling moved from the BOAC Airways Terminal at Victoria to Stafford Court, Kensington. At last, BEA had a home of its own in London to deal separately with its swelling tide of passengers. The new terminal was named Kensington Air Station. The supplies depot at White Waltham, Berkshire, was moved to Wembley, Middlesex.

But there was hardly time to lay the last carpet before another major job came BEA's way. Russia had imposed a blockade on surface communications between Germany's Western zone and its old capital—the Berlin airlift was about to begin. It started on 27th July 1948 with the Allied Air Forces using every available plane to ferry vital supplies

Proud flutter of flags on the south side of Northolt, 1951

16

in to the besieged city. By 4th August BEA had been asked to step in and organise the British independent airlines which had offered their help.

It was a massive operation. A total of 25 tiny British airlines spent the next year flying daily to Berlin. Acting as agents for the Foreign Office, BEA kept the planes flying from aerodromes in West Germany. Engineers and handlers had to find spares for and overcome the eccentricities of DC-3 Dakotas, Haltons, Lancastrians, Liberators, Tudors, Hythes, Bristol freighters and Yorks. At the end of it all the civilian fleet had taken in 146,980 tons of essential supplies, using 103 aircraft which made a total of 22,000 trips.

The airlift was a huge success, but BEA's general position was far from comfortable. It lost well over £8 million in three years and although passengers, freight and mail increased, more staff cuts were forced on the unhappy board of directors. There were rows, resignations and then changes. Marshal of the Royal Air Force Lord Douglas of Kirtleside became chairman. The order for Ambassadors remained, but contracts were also signed for the Viscount, the world's first propeller-turbine powered aircraft. These two events, coupled with the start of services from London (Heathrow) airport, were to revolutionise the corporation.

Northolt had been birthplace, cradle and nursery of BEA. In its heyday it was the busiest airport in Europe and it was still dealing with more passengers and planes than Heathrow in 1952. BEA was responsible for 83 per cent of the traffic through Northolt which virtually closed overnight when the corporation moved to Heathrow in 1954.

The last commercial service to run from Northolt was on 30th October 1954 when G–AHCZ Royal Mail Aircraft 'Charles Samson'—a BEA DC-3 Dakota now called a Pionair—left in the gathering gloom for Jersey. In eight years BEA flew some two million passengers between Northolt and the Continent and another million on Channel Islands flights. Many more had been through the airport on domestic services. Three-quarters of the 300,000 flights into and out of Northolt in those eight years had been made by BEA.

But the nest had become too small . . .

18

CHAPTER 2

ON THE MOVE

BEA BROUGHT the world to London and no wonder schoolboys and curious onlookers gathered around the boundary fences of the two airports on warm evenings to watch passengers leaving the planes. Visitors to Britain came with Paris hats, Lisbon baskets and the whiff of Spanish cigarettes. Arabs from the Middle East shuffled by in sandals. Fur-booted Scandinavians humped the bulk of three kilograms of extra clothing which they were allowed on flights to and from the Baltic. Accents mingled, skins were every shade and the famous were seen striding along with the anonymous.

On other BEA stations in the British Isles the sights were more usual. There was nothing foreign about the booking agent in the lonely Hebridean Island of Barra. Mr Macpherson looked every inch a native in his sailor's peaked cap, tweed jacket and gumboots. At Glasgow's Renfrew airport, the new manager would don the kilt for special occasions and there was nothing unusual in that. Down in the Scilly Isles, passengers on the regular run to Land's End got used to seeing Mrs Simmonds, aged 79, and Mrs Addison, aged 82, stepping aboard the morning plane to go shopping. It was the same at Liverpool's Speke airport and in the Isle of Man. But Jersey did own to greeting a few strangers such as Prince Bira and Raymond

Mays when it was time for the annual international road race in the Channel Islands.

When the Jupiters and Avro 19s had been withdrawn, some of the domestic outposts were once again linked by the Dragon Rapide biplanes, also known as Dominies, DH89s, or Islanders. They had a cruising speed of 132 mph and a range of 578 miles, enough to do all the jobs BEA asked of them. But a cabin holding six to eight passengers was not big enough; wherever possible the 32-seat Dakotas were sent in as replacements.

BEA's only fear was that the Dakota might not be accepted by the regions. Scathing comments had been relayed back to London about the German Jupiters and it was feared the DC-3 from America might meet a similar hostility. But the Daks were roomy and reliable. Safety, speed and space were the requirements—and they could provide all three.

It was of small interest to those working out of London that the big move for BEA was about to begin. The distance was an insignificant few miles and it made no difference if you were out of town. All the airlines were cashing in on a boom in passenger flights and it was no longer possible to tolerate two separate airports attempting to operate side by side at full throttle. Northolt was hemmed

Night at London Airport, Heathrow, 1957

in by the A40 trunk road, housing estates and BEA's Keyline House complex. There was room for expansion at Heathrow. BEA's first scheduled flight from the new base, known as London Airport until the emergence of Gatwick, came on 16th April when a Viking left for Paris. But only 21,000 of BEA's passengers went through London airport in 1950 compared with 542,000 from Northolt.

The first cheap off-peak night fares had already been introduced, but increasing the number of passengers was not the airline's main concern. Devaluation and an increase in petrol tax had sent the cost of flying spiralling. Staff cuts had cracked the confidence of those who were kept on and BEA was fully aware that British South American Airways, the sister corporation formed on the same day, had just been wound up and its assets absorbed by BOAC.

BSAA had failed largely because of its fleet of Tudor IVs. Two had been lost in fine weather and their fate could not be explained. One had disappeared in the West Atlantic, another crashed in the Caribbean. Soon afterwards, a Tudor V crashed in Wales. The remainder of the fleet was withdrawn. Against this background it was not easy for BEA's pilots, engineers and maintenance men to look forward with complete confidence to the introduction of new aircraft. BEA's new management was determined to look on the bright side. Chairman Lord Douglas of Kirtleside even saw a ray of sunshine in a forecast loss of £1,450,000. 'I believe that with no further blows like devaluation and the increased petrol tax we shall beat the estimated deficit,' he said.

It was not exactly a subject to cheer about, but it was better than nothing. And his lordship was right—the loss turned out to be £87,000 smaller than the forecast.

The first of BEA's new aircraft was to be the Ambassador —larger, faster and more sophisticated than the Viking. The fleet in March 1950 was made up of 42 Vikings, 24 passenger DC-3s, 6 DC-3 freighters and 20 Rapides. The 20 Ambassadors had pressurised cabins so that they could fly above the storms. And they were the first BEA planes to stand horizontally on tricycle undercarriages which had the third 'balancing' wheel under the nose instead of the tail. Pilots could now see what was in front of them when taxiing and passengers no longer had to climb uphill on a sloping floor.

Like most new types of aircraft, the Ambassador did not arrive on time. There were snags with its engines, undercarriage and flying controls. Two prototypes were tried and scrapped. The third was made to measure for BEA but it, too, was behind schedule.

Fortunately, the airline had not put all its eggs in one basket. Contracts were under negotiation for two other types. One was the Marathon, but it was not big enough. The other promised to be something special. The Vickers Viscount prototype was loaned to BEA by Vickers-Armstrongs and on 29th July 1950 it made history by operating the world's first service by a turbine-propeller driven aircraft. It was a bold move by Vickers and BEA —equivalent today to BOAC borrowing a Concorde for a couple of weeks and showing it off on the New York run.

The Viscount V.630 prototype, forerunner of the mass-produced versions which were to sell all over the world, was returned to Vickers after four weeks. It was another 18 months before BEA was able to introduce the plane in large numbers.

Lord Douglas had appointed as his chief executive Mr Peter Masefield who was 35 and an enthusiast for any kind of flying. Under Mr Masefield were an equally energetic and youthful bunch of executives who included the airline's two future chairmen, Sir Anthony Milward and Mr Henry Marking. Such was the spirit of BEA at this time that some of the board members gave up part of their salaries to help the financial crisis and Mr Masefield cut his own earnings.

The airline was anxious to get started with the Ambassador, despite reports that it had been seen on flight trials with two slightly different engines and odd undercarriage legs. The Airspeed Company was absorbed

Construction at Heathrow: the first scheduled BEA flight from this airport was on April 16, 1950

21

by de Havillands and the modified airliner began its test programme backed by the long experience of its new owners. There were still faults, however. BEA introduced it to the public on 3rd September 1951 but was forced to withdraw it again for more alterations. There was a renewed determination, however, to show that buying British was the right policy and like a jockey spurring and cajoling his mount, BEA's insistence pushed the plane into becoming a reliable and comfortable money-maker.

A new Elizabethan era was about to begin with the succession of Her Majesty the Queen and the Ambassador was renamed 'Elizabethan'. For once the name was to become universally accepted. Part of the reason was that only 23 of these aircraft were ever built and BEA operated 20 of them.

As always, the new planes were shown off on the prestige routes. The Elizabethan began on the London–Paris service on 13th March 1952, five years after the first prototype had flown. The route to Paris was along 'Amber One', code name for the main air corridor to Europe. It was a highway which BEA pilots already knew well and one which has remained the most important on the network. It is the busiest international air route in the world and at the same time one of the shortest.

Flying BEA's 'Silver Wing' service to Paris by Elizabethan became the most fashionable and elegant way of travelling. It was the air equivalent to the Golden Arrow train service or crossing the Atlantic in the *Queen Elizabeth*. BEA was still losing a million pounds a year but the glamorous Silver Wing service glossed over the fact. Special Silver Wing coaches collected passengers from Kensington Air Station and made the best of the 50-minute journey along the Bath Road to the airport. Once in the air, however, it was four miles a minute in a pressurised cabin and lunches of champagne, Scotch salmon, grilled lamb cutlets and Cape pears in port wine.

Frowns melted into smiles and BEA's morale rose with every flight. Breakfast in London and lunch in Paris cost £15 19s (£15·95) return. And three of the crew of six were there to give their undivided attention to the passengers.

Each of the Elizabethans was named after a famous figure in the reign of Elizabeth 1st. Reproductions of the signatures of Sir Richard Grenville, William Shakespeare, Sir Francis Drake, Lord Burghley and others were displayed in the passenger cabins. One plane was christened 'Christopher Marlowe', but the dramatist's autograph was difficult to obtain. The search lasted several months before the autograph hunters checked through the dusty deeds at Canterbury Probate Record Office at Maidstone, Kent, and found the signature—on Marlowe's will.

The Elizabethan was an easy aircraft to fly and passengers liked the unobstructed view made possible by the position of the wings mounted high on the fuselage. BEA had carried its first five million passengers by 30th October 1952, but it was still losing millions and was to need all the appeal of the Elizabethans and the new Viscounts to get it out of the red.

The Viscount prototype, the V.630, first flew on 16th July 1948. Arguments raged among BEA's board members about the new airliner. It was obviously too small and it used a means of propulsion which had never been tried in a passenger-carrying plane. It was the first commercial aircraft in the world to have part jet and part propeller driven engines as distinct from the conventional piston engines.

Fortunately for the Viscount and BEA, the conservative element of the board did not include Lord Douglas. By August 1950 a firm order for 20 Viscounts was placed. The V.630 prototype was hired and used on BEA's Northolt–Le Bourget, Paris route from 29th July 1950 for two weeks for prestige and publicity purposes. Then it popped up from Northolt to Edinburgh's Turnhouse airport on a regular run between 15–23 August, stealing some of the limelight from the Edinburgh Festival. If the passengers failed to understand the principle of the new engines it did not matter. It was enough to be flying at 275 mph and 20,000 feet.

Left: in the sky, an Elizabethan. On the ground a Viscount in Heathrow's engineering base

Above: de-icing at Heathrow, January, 1950

Right: not the Antarctic, but snowbound Heathrow, 1955

In 26 days the plane completed 127 flying hours and carried 1,815 passengers. Later versions would carry more than 70 people at a time but the V.630 had only 32 seats. There was no doubting its popularity; it could scarcely have failed to please. The seats were roomy and comfortable and were set as far apart as first class seats are today.

Huge oval windows gave the passengers a panoramic view.

Exactly two years after its excursion with BEA, the V.630 was written off at Khartoum, much to the dismay of aviation historians who would have preserved the plane for ever. But V.630 did not come home. The undercarriage collapsed during a simulated forced landing in the Sahara

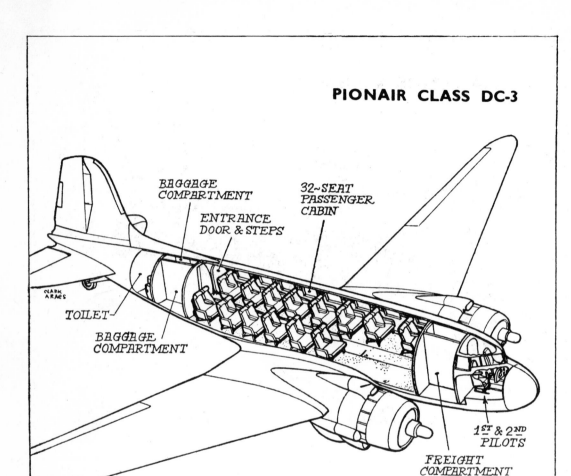

PIONAIR CLASS DC-3

BAGGAGE COMPARTMENT

ENTRANCE DOOR & STEPS

32~SEAT PASSENGER CABIN

CLARK ARAES

TOILET

BAGGAGE COMPARTMENT

1ST & 2ND PILOTS

FREIGHT COMPARTMENT

and the plane slid to an undignified and inglorious end on its belly.

A strange and rare bird appeared in BEA's colours in 1953.

The captain of an Elizabethan almost fell out of his seat on a flight from Amsterdam to Northolt one hazy afternoon. Nervously he indicated to his co-pilot, testing him to see if it was a mirage which he had just seen. Shooting along over the clouds was a DC-3 Dakota, miles higher than one had ever been before and travelling at an unusually high speed. The BEA captain was about to make an emergency radio call to report his discovery when he noticed the DC-3's engines. They were long and slim, not at all like the familiar stubby piston engines seen on thousands of Dakotas all over the world.

The plane was a Dart-Dakota, an ordinary DC-3 fitted with the cigar-shaped Rolls-Royce Dart turbo-prop engines. BEA had converted two of its fleet to act as flying

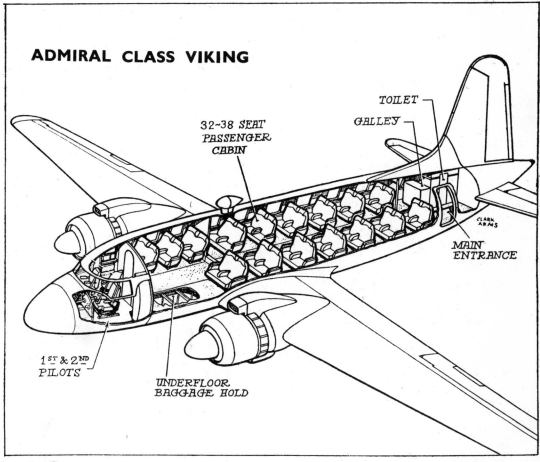

ADMIRAL CLASS VIKING

32~38 SEAT
PASSENGER
CABIN

TOILET
GALLEY

MAIN
ENTRANCE

CLARK
ARMS

1ST & 2ND
PILOTS

UNDERFLOOR
BAGGAGE HOLD

testbeds for the engines which were to power the Viscount. While Vickers were 'stretching' the fuselage to build into it BEA's demand for more seats, the DC-3 was testing the stamina of the engines. BEA was in a hurry for its new airliner.

The Dart-Dakota was an outstanding example of co-operation between airline and manufacturer, almost unique in the history of aviation. The principle of trying out new engines on older aircraft is now widely used. A Vulcan bomber first flew the Olympus 593 for Concorde and a VC10 had two of its Conway jets removed to accommodate and test a Rolls-Royce RB211 engine.

The Dart-Dakota was put to good use. The two planes converted by BEA were cargo carriers and climbing to unprecedented heights at greatly increased speeds, they became the fastest freighters in the business. From the pilot's point of view it was an entirely new aircraft. The greatest difficulty experienced elsewhere was a name for it.

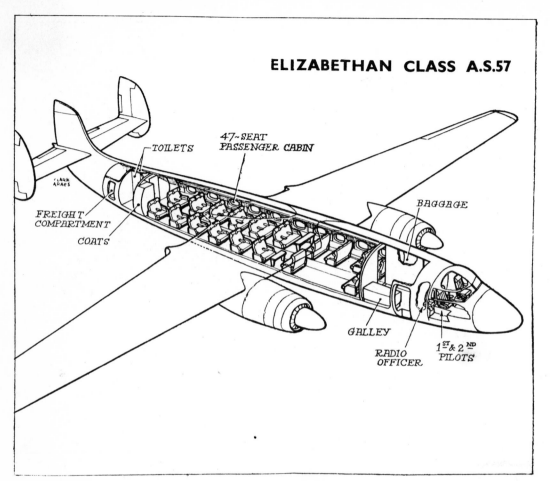

ELIZABETHAN CLASS A.S.57

47~SEAT
PASSENGER CABIN

TOILETS

CLARK
ARMS

BAGGAGE

FREIGHT
COMPARTMENT

COATS

GALLEY

RADIO
OFFICER

1ST & 2ND
PILOTS

Interior of the Elizabethan. Note the rear-facing seats

Basically, it was a Douglas DC-3 Dakota. BEA had re-named its fleet 'Pionairs' and called them 'Pionair-Leopards' when they were used for freight. Would these two rare birds, to be correct, now have to be called Douglas DC-3 Dart-Dakota Pionair-Leopards? Add to that their individual names 'Sir Henry Royce' and 'Claude Johnson' and it became quite a mouthful. Most people settled for the term Dart-Dakota.

Amid the mudheaps, raw concrete and bulldozers of the growing London airport, the first sustained schedule of flights by Viscounts began in April 1953. Three-quarters of BEA's London flights were still anchored at Northolt, but the prestige service were now going down 'Amber One' to the Continent from the new base. The limelight had been captured by BOAC which began the world's first pure jet services with the first generation of Comets. Tragically, this lead for Britain's long-haul airline and the country's aircraft industry was wiped out when three Comets crashed

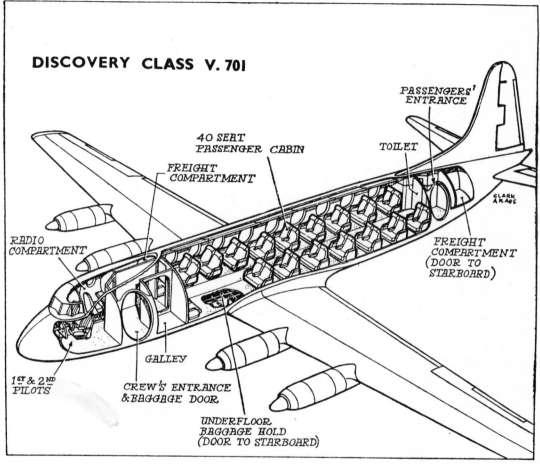

Viscount interior, with all seats forward-facing

DISCOVERY CLASS V. 701

PASSENGERS' ENTRANCE

40 SEAT PASSENGER CABIN

TOILET

FREIGHT COMPARTMENT

RADIO COMPARTMENT

FREIGHT COMPARTMENT (DOOR TO STARBOARD)

CLARK ARAOS

1ST & 2ND PILOTS

GALLEY

CREW'S ENTRANCE & BAGGAGE DOOR

UNDERFLOOR BAGGAGE HOLD (DOOR TO STARBOARD)

in quick succession. The remainder of the fleet was grounded and it was years later when the fault was traced to metal fatigue which caused cracks in the pressurised hull.

The Viscount, meanwhile, was a huge success. BEA's order for 20 Viscount V.701s was the first placed by a nationally owned corporation for the supply of a new type of aircraft. BEA had confidence in its own judgement and the introduction of the new plane could not have come at a better time. Seven poor years had made BEA something of a joke. Only once had the annual deficit been less than a million pounds.

There is no doubt that the Viscount would never have received so much attention or scored such a brilliant success later on if it had not been for the way BEA supported it. Without the corporation's demand for more seats and other improvements, Vickers would have gone ahead with original plans and produced smaller planes.

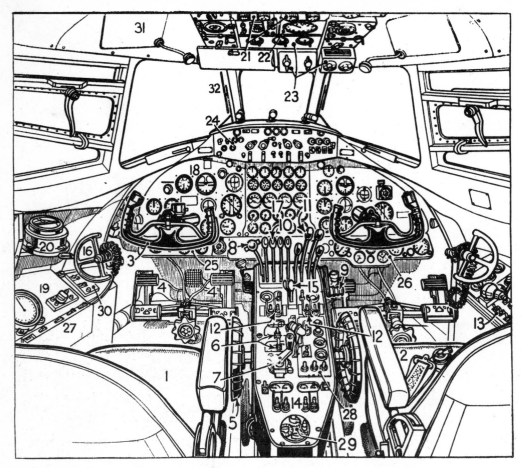

THE VISCOUNT CONTROL PANEL

1. Captain's seat
2. First Officer's seat

FLYING CONTROLS
*3. Control column (incorporating aileron and elevator controls and handbrake for undercarriage main wheels)
*4. Rudder pedals (with toe brakes for undercarriage main wheels)
*5. Elevator trim wheel
6. Aileron trim switches
7. Rudder trim unit

8. Flap control
9. Control locking lever

ENGINE CONTROLS
10. Throttles
11. High pressure fuel cocks
12. Low pressure fuel cocks
13. Fuel controls
14. Fuel trimmers

UNDERCARRIAGE CONTROLS
15. Undercarriage lever
*16. Nosewheel steering wheel

MAIN INSTRUMENTS
17. Engine gauges
*18. Instrument flying panel
19. CL2 compass master indicator
20. Magnetic compass
21. VHF radio control knobs
22. Automatic direction finding equipment
23. Decca navigator equipment

ANCILLARY CONTROLS
24. Panel for propeller feathering buttons, fire warning lights and switches, fuel flowmeters, etc.
25. Panel for undercarriage indicators, flap indicator, etc.
26. Panel for fuel contents gauges and rate of fuel flow indicators
27. Cockpit lighting controls
28. Automatic pilot
29. Sperry zero reader controls
*30. Radio selector switches

ACCESSORIES
*31. Sun visor
*32. Windscreen wiper

* These items are duplicated on port and starboard sides

The staff – ground and air – needed to keep one Viscount in service

31

VIP treatment for Sir Winston Churchill, returning to London from Catania in a Viscount, April, 1955

The main concourse in the South East Passenger Building at Heathrow   *The BEA Flight Operations Centre at Heathrow*

As it was the Viscount became the best-selling aircraft in Europe.

The early prestige flights had an impact on Air France, traditional rival to Britain's airlines in Europe. Their order for twelve Viscounts came a little more than a year after BEA had signed up for the plane. Aer Lingus, by this time beginning to go its own way, quickly followed suit and so did other airlines in North America. Sixteen airlines were flying the British turbo-prop by 1955.

Blueprints for the Viscount were drawn up in 1946. The makers at first chose the name 'Viceroy' but changed their minds before the first flight. BEA made an unsuccessful attempt to change the name to 'Discovery'.

Everything seemed to be happening at once for BEA in 1953. The pick of the new aircraft carried in processions of distinguished visitors for the coronation. Kensington Air Station was considered too small and closed after exactly five years. The new London centre was Waterloo Air Terminal, a building erected originally for the Festival of Britain. Tourist fares were introduced for the first time on European routes and another passenger milestone, 1½ million in a year, was passed.

By October BEA was preparing to embark on one of the longest ever prestige and publicity ventures ever attempted. The coronation was over but everyone seemed to want to go on waving their flags. The event was an air race, arranged by the residents of Christchurch, New Zealand, as part of a centenary celebration. Chief executive Peter Masefield was to be team manager of a 'Viscount XI', an entry which had the Government's blessing. The plane was the V.700, third of the Viscount prototypes which had been named 'Endeavour'.

BEA set about the planning with relish. 'Endeavour' was on loan from the Ministry of Supply so there would be no interruption of the airline's schedules while mechanics tinkered with it. The whole exercise was to be paid for by the ministry, much to the relief of BEA's board. Teams of engineers worked up the four Dart engines to get every ounce of power out of them while three of the airline's captains, two radio officers, a navigator, two technicians from Vickers and one from Rolls-Royce got their heads together over maps, diagrams and piles of flight manuals. Four large fuel tanks were built into the fuselage and unwanted seats stripped out.

Planning the Britain to New Zealand Air Race, in 1953. Members of the BEA race crew discuss the route at a pre-flight briefing. From the left: Captain W. Baillie, pilot in command; Mr. Peter Masefield, Chief Executive of BEA and team manager; Captain A. S. Johnson, pilot; Chief Radio Officer, I. A. Dagliesh (back to camera); Mr. R. H. Chadwick, navigation officer; Captain S. E. Jones, pilot; and radio officer E. H. S. Bristow

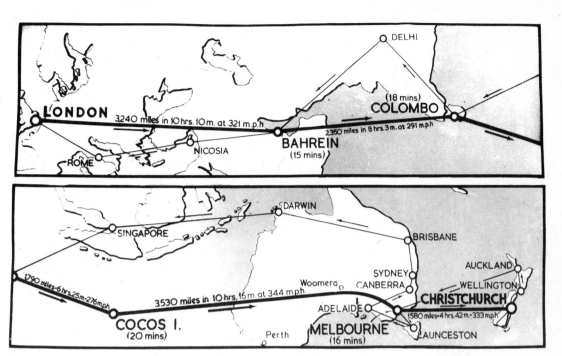

Map showing flight times of the BEA Viscount which took part in the New Zealand race. The plane covered 12,490 miles in 40 hours 45 minutes – an average speed of 316 mph

In this racing condition, 'Endeavour' could carry 2,900 gallons of fuel and fly 3,500 miles nonstop. Newsreel cameramen clinging to their tripods on the tops of their cars recorded the moment as the plane lifted from London airport's main runway towards the afternoon sun. Its rivals were a Douglas DC-6 entered by KLM Royal Dutch Airlines and a Handley Page Hastings of the Royal New Zealand Air Force. The handicap formula used by the Royal Aero Club was severe and gave the Viscount no chance of winning its section. It finished the course hours ahead of its rivals and the BEA team was placed second behind the KLM crew.

The times set up by 'Endeavour' established the first of the Viscount's many world records. One by one the reports of the plane's progress were radioed back to BEA's headquarters where an all-night staff plotted the position on a map. A bare 15 minutes on the ground at Bahrein to refuel, 18 minutes at Colombo, 20 minutes at the Cocos Islands in the Indian Ocean. Then came a remarkable nonstop section of 3,530 miles to Melbourne which lasted ten hours 16 minutes and was completed at an average speed of 343 mph. The total time to Melbourne was 35 hours 47 minutes (faster than the overall times for today's jet timetables) and half the previous best time. Sixteen minutes in Australia and the Viscount was airborne again, reaching its final destination at Christchurch after a total elapsed time of 40 hours 45 minutes. This gave an average speed of 316 mph for the course of 12,490 miles.

Mr Masefield led his weary team from the aircraft. There had been makeshift bunks inside the Viscount but the team was too excited to sleep. They included chief flight captain W. 'Bill' Baillie and Parliamentary Secretary to the Ministry of Transport and Civil Aviation, Mr John Profumo, who had acted as steward. A full demonstration

Captain W. Baillie (left), pilot in command of the BEA Viscount and Mr. Peter Masefield, team manager of the BEA New Zealand Air Race crew

over 1,000 miles. BOAC looked after the long haul routes out of Britain and BEA's work was mainly on journeys of less than 500 miles. The Elizabethan was more profitable than the Viscount on legs up to 400 miles, but a 'new' plane was needed for the 400–900 mile range.

An order for the V.802 version of the Viscount was placed even before the New Zealand Air Race had been completed. The V.802 could carry a maximum of 65 passengers and was at its best on trips of 600–800 miles. Better still, it had the flexibility to fill in on both longer and shorter routes when required.

BEA had learned the hard way that hardly anyone wanted to fly across Europe in winter. The number of passengers carried between November and February doubled in July, August and September. Part of the reason was the way bad weather wrecked winter timetables, sometimes for days on end with a pea-soup fog descending on London.

Ten whole working days were lost in the three winter months of 1952/3 because of fog, snow and ice. The new Viscount could adapt and beat these conditions. Seats could be taken out during the winter and the aircraft re-scheduled for cargo flights. Adjusting to the demand, it could carry some passengers and be fitted out to accommodate freight in the remaining space. A large door was built in at the front and the floor strengthened so that motor-car sized crates could be loaded. Meal galleys mounted on rails could be slid into position depending on the size of the passenger cabin.

The ambitious plans and expansion in all directions allowed BEA to make a profit over the summer months. But it was swamped by losses in the winter. In his Christmas message to the staff in 1954, Lord Douglas wrote, 'The Promised Land of profits still eludes us.' Viscounts were bringing in 38 per cent of BEA's revenue and the airline could not wait to get more of them.

Almost any scheme was given a try in order to help cure the continuing financial crisis. During the slack winter

programme of the new plane was made in the following three weeks in New Zealand, Australia and Asia. The aircraft was flown to 31 cities and towns spending 118 hours in the air and covering 31,977 miles.

The Viscount had arrived, yet BEA was not happy with the first batch of Discovery class V.700s. They could carry only 47 passengers and were most profitable on journeys

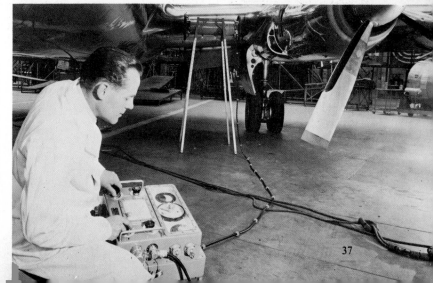

Above: de-icing a BEA Viscount at Heathrow. Right: using radiographic equipment at BEA's engineering base at Heathrow

months, pilots were invited to sell tickets. More than 40 seasoned aviators were selected to spend their non-flying duty hours approaching industrial firms and travel agents to win new business. The flying salesmen were to have two weeks at a time on the road and then return for flying practice. But where was the sense in it? More than a million passengers a year were going BEA on international flights and the airline was the second largest international carrier in the world behind Pan-American Airways.

BEA had enough passengers, but it was spending too

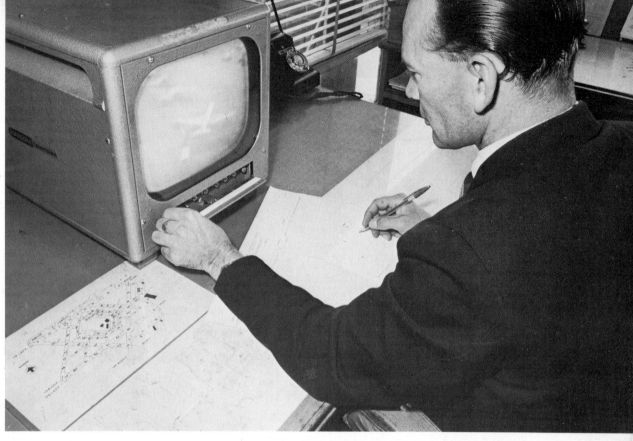

Left: Viscount at Heathrow, showing the new markings adopted by BEA in 1959

Right: using closed-circuit TV at Heathrow

much in transporting them and providing uneconomic services. Yet the thirst for more business was not quenched. Glossy picture postcards of the snow-capped Matterhorn were sent out from Zermatt by BEA representatives. Each carried a genuine Swiss stamp franked in the correct manner. Ten thousand of the cards were posted to men and women at various London addresses, chosen at random from telephone directories. The cards bore the message:

'October 30th 1954. I am enjoying my stay in Switzerland, marvellous food and scenery. Flew B.E.A. Viscount to Zurich, only 2 hours, returning Viscount from Geneva. Wonderful views of the Matterhorn, good to know such exciting places are so near home. Best wishes, Jack.'

In no time at all a posse of angry husbands were ringing BEA ready to round up the renegade 'Jack'. He may have been all right in Switzerland, but there were heated arguments at the homes of some of the women who received the mysterious cards. The callers were told by a BEA official that the cards were part of a campaign to get more traffic on flights to Switzerland. He went on:

'If you look very closely at the handwritten message on the postcard you will see it is *printed*, although it may look like ordinary ink. The same person who wrote the original also wrote the names and addresses in ink, but by hand.'

BEA decided it was time to leave home, anyway. London airport was now dealing with twice as many passengers as Northolt could handle at its peak. At the same time the Viking was scrapped. For seven years it had competed for BEA on the international routes and at one stage the airline had a fleet of 49. The Vikings covered 65½ million miles for BEA transporting nearly three million passengers and earning £35 million. But they could not survive against the popular Elizabethans and the dazzling success of the sleek Viscounts.

The airline had entered a new era. London–Paris flights alone were carrying more than a quarter of a million passengers a year. The London–Jersey route was next busiest with 126,000 and London to Glasgow and Belfast close behind. Financially, the corner was turned. After eight years of heavy losses a profit of £63,039 was recorded in 1955. It was greeted with sighs of relief. A staggering total of 15½ million pounds had been lost since 1946. Chief executive Peter Masefield told the 9,000 employees:

'BEA can hold up its head as a profitable undertaking in the most difficult of all air transport fields—the short-haul, highly-seasonal business.'

Lord Douglas said it was a 'rigorous control of expenditure combined with a highly successful sales drive' that had made profits possible. Even 'Jack's' postcards had helped.

The move to London airport did not appear to have affected the airline. The telling factor had been the introduction of the Viscount. When it came, DC-3s and other smaller aircraft were released to do the more specialised jobs where they, too, could make money. The Viscount blanketed European services offering smooth comfort, speed and luxury. BEA went on buying them and later versions were even more successful. It has flown a total of 79 Viscounts, some of which are being used today.

Much of the credit for its success was due to the designer Sir George Edwards, who later became chairman of the British Aircraft Corporation. He had the backing from the start of Peter Masefield. On the crest of a wave, Mr Masefield left BEA in 1955 to become chairman of the Bristol Aircraft Company. The second phase in the rise of BEA was over. Designer and promoter were pictured together on the steps of a Viscount by a magazine in May 1955. The editor saw fit to caption the photograph 'Makers of Aviation History'.

The ASMA radar equipment (foreground) in Heathrow's control tower

41

CHAPTER 3

TAKE-OFF

MORE AND MORE destinations in Europe had to be served by BEA as the major cities recovered from the war and tourism grew. The airline was stretching as far as the Iron Curtain by the end of the fifties. The storms, boiling sun and arctic snows of three continents were everyday hazards. Routes went as far as North Africa and Beirut in the South and East and up to the edge of the Arctic Circle in the North. Servicing an airliner in a sandstorm or getting spares out to places like Benghazi and Cairo were formidable problems. So were the blizzards in Norway, where engineers undertook the rebuilding of a damaged Viscount at Oslo in the middle of winter. Thick snow lay on the ground and as there was no hangar available, an 'igloo' was constructed with wood and canvas over the wing joints and middle section of the fuselage. It allowed a shivering band of technicians to continue to work on the plane. The sub-zero temperatures were kept out with mechanical heaters and in two months the plane was back in service.

More than ten million passengers had been carried on BEA planes when Mr Masefield left the airline. Lord Douglas combined his job with that of chief executive and then appointed Mr Anthony Milward (who was knighted in 1966) as his right-hand man. Mr Milward was controller of operations at the end of 1955 when he had to warn the staff that repairs and modifications had depleted the airline's fleet. The result was nearly a commercial disaster. Some of the staff were ready to announce that BEA could not carry all the passengers who had booked with the corporation.

The only alternative to leaving them stranded was to carry passengers in aircraft chartered from outside. Engineers warned the controller of operations that delays were inevitable. Time had to be taken in checking planes between flights. Safety regulations had to be observed even if they did make planes late. Mr Milward told his staff:

'We must recognise one hard fact, that an airline's reputation stands or falls largely on punctuality and regularity. Our customers pay money for the speed of air transport and are understandably annoyed by unpunctuality. It is a problem we *must* solve.'

Thousands of businessmen now flew with BEA. They were beginning to grumble about the airline like others did on the railways. A total of 81 per cent of BEA's flights arrived on time in 1954, but only 77 per cent the following year. The problem had not been solved ten years later when a special log of flights between London and Glasgow was kept by BEA at the request of *The Times* newspaper. The route was then the busiest in Britain with 17 flights a day operated by jets and turbo-props.

Left: preparing a Vanguard for take-off under severe conditions

The worst delay on take-off was ten minutes, and no plane was more than 16 minutes late on arrival. Most of the flights *to* Glasgow arrived up to five minutes late because of head-winds. Those on the southward journey which were not delayed on take-off by incoming aircraft, arrived early.

Even after 25 years, a final solution has not emerged. Retiring chairman Sir Anthony Milward began another campaign against the 'creeping and infectious disease' of unpunctuality as he was leaving in 1970.

The accent was on good service in the late fifties, but it was hard to please two million passengers a year. Damages of £30 each were awarded to a company chairman and his wife in a case against BEA and Air France over a Paris–London flight. The two airlines were operating an agreement which allowed passengers holding tickets for one airline to be carried if necessary by the other. The aggrieved couple boarded a plane at Orly airport and were looking forward to a champagne luncheon as advertised. But a double-booking had been made and they were transferred to the next plane. It also meant changing airlines and instead of lunch they were served tea, buns and slab cake.

The important thing for BEA was to learn from such mistakes. An incentive scheme was started under which cash payments of between £2 and £500 were offered for ideas to any member of the 10,000 staff. The first award of £500 went to Mr Kenneth Wilkinson, the schedules planning manager (now deputy chief executive), for an idea on saving fuel. A further £250 bonus was paid to a second man for adapting the theory and putting it into practice. BEA had given away £750 and saved thousands.

The slim profit now being made by BEA was trimmed in 1957 by the Suez crisis which slashed traffic on the lucrative Athens–Cairo route. The service of three flights a week had to stop and with them went an income of £200,000 a year. Increases in petrol tax took another

Continued on page 53

Thumbs up from the captain, and his Trident Two is ready for take off

BEA's Comet 4B carries up to a hundred passengers. It was introduced in April, 1960

Continued from page 44

£184,000—tankers had to come the long way round from the Middle East oilfields. Nor did it help the corporation's cause when independent airlines began 'stealing' holiday-makers heading for Spain.

The transfer to temporary buildings at West London Air Terminal at Cromwell Road, Kensington, was an additional but necessary expense. Coach journeys to London airport were cut from 65 to 40 minutes. Twenty-two sites had been visited before BEA decided to move from the Waterloo Air Terminal. The new base was to have been occupied by BEA, BOAC and independent British airlines, but plans were changed and BEA became the sole tenants.

In 1963 Prince Philip opened the permanent buildings on the same site. It was the end of 15 years of wandering across the West End of London. The terminal is dominated by a huge block 130 feet high, containing 75,000 tons of concrete and 120,000 square feet of glass. It stands on a four-acre triangle of land bounded by the railway lines of London's underground system. It was just as well that BEA was the only airline to move in—today there is no room for others. At one stage BEA had six offices scattered across London. The terminal brought them all together.

The boom in the airline business around the world in 1957 caused a shortage of pilots. BEA's position was made worse by the retirement of many ex-R.A.F. fliers who had joined in 1946. A travelling selection board toured Commonwealth countries and rounded up volunteers. Then the R.A.F. helped out by releasing a considerable number of pilots. With a defence policy leaning towards missiles, the services needed far fewer pilots and the R.A.F. was glad of the chance to place some elsewhere.

Eager to keep its fleet up to date, BEA decided to withdraw its Elizabethans from scheduled services. The Viscount had overshadowed all other propeller-drive planes to such an extent that BEA scrapped plans for the successful Elizabethans after the first order for 20. They had taken five years to develop and stayed in service for only six. They carried a total of $2\frac{1}{2}$ million BEA passengers. At Christmas 1957 the corporation still had 13 along with 38 DC-3s, three Rapides, 25 Viscount V701s, 22 V.802s and eight of the very latest V806s. The plan was to convert all international services to Viscount flights.

The last scheduled run by an Elizabethan was made in July, 1958. Five months earlier one of the fleet had been involved in an accident which shook commercial aviation and the whole of Europe. The Manchester United Football Club was returning after a cup match in Germany. It was a bitter February day with a carpet of snow on the ground and more in the air.

The Manchester team and a number of journalists boarded the BEA Elizabethan 'Lord Burghley' at Munich. Twice the crew attempted take-offs, but the engines seemed to lack power at the critical moment. The third attempt ended in disaster although the plane never lifted off the runway. It ploughed through the perimeter fence, hitting trees and a house. Many of the 23 killed were famous footballers who were in current international teams. Some of those who died were well-known sportswriters, some were officials of the celebrated club.

There had been worse air disasters in terms of numbers killed, but none received the amount of publicity which followed the Munich crash. It was BEA's eleventh fatal accident involving a passenger carrying aircraft. Five of these, including two mid-air collisions, occurred in the primitive flying conditions which existed in the forties.

In this darkest hour BEA's objective was to learn from the tragedy so that it might never happen again. Munich and many other accidents before it occurred because of unseen and unknown hazards. Metal fatigue had hardly been studied, and clear air turbulence is still a mystery today. Faults in design sometimes allowed parts to be assembled incorrectly and this led to accidents. Harmless nuts and bolts could be lethal if they were dropped by accident into parts of the fuselage or wings where vibration could shake them into jamming a control. One plane caught

The first Vanguard to Glasgow from Heathrow waits for its passengers as the sun struggles through the fog (December, 1962)

Munich disaster, one in a mid-air collision and another by sabotage. Airlines do not boast of safety records. A clean sheet can be ruined without the airline being at fault. BEA's record is worse than some, better than others, but it is almost impossible to find the truth from statistics. The Elizabethans had flown nearly 30 million miles in complete safety before Munich. Many of the aircraft continued in service with other airlines long after BEA had sold them.

The corporation's problem after the disaster was to sustain its expansion. There were new routes to be opened up and the faster planes allowed re-scheduling and time-table changes. Not one of the 50 or so destinations across Europe was more than half a day away. Flying times had been slashed.

A comparison of travelling times between airports from London, shown in hours and minutes, for 1947 and 1958 revealed:

	1947	**1958**
Amsterdam	1 20	1 05
Athens	11 05	6 35
Berlin	4 45	3 25
Copenhagen	3 20	2 25
Gibraltar	7 55	4 20
Hamburg	2 55	1 55
Istanbul	26 30	8 50
Lisbon	7 00	4 00
Oslo	5 00	2 55
Paris	1 30	1 05
Rome	6 30	3 20
Stockholm	5 25	4 35
Vienna	6 00	3 05

The times include stop-overs in some cases.

fire and crashed soon after take-off because its wheels had got too hot from prolonged fast taxiing.

Very few crashes were correctly blamed on 'pilot error', the two most overworked words in official reports. Extensive tests were made after the Munich crash which was originally put down to negligence by the captain. The first of the new tests could prove only that ice on the wings was *not* the cause. Over the course of ten years the theory emerged that pools of slush and melting snow on the runway had slowed the Elizabethan at the critical moment when it was accelerating towards a take-off. BEA was cleared by the British Government.

BEA has lost five aircraft in the 13 years since the

The success of the turbo-prop Viscounts had forced BEA into going all out for this kind of aircraft. Elizabethans were being sold and the DC-3 was outdated. More new planes had to be found. BEA had taken delivery by

1958 of all but one of the 79 Viscounts it was to operate. It was looking forward to the Vanguard. A profit of over a million pounds had been made and there was at last money to spend. Eighty per cent of BEA's passengers were being flown in Viscounts and the Vanguard was to be bigger, better and faster.

Nothing had been left to chance. The Vanguard had to be right. At the beginning of 1957 sixteen BEA pilots—half nominated by the airline and half by the British Air Line Pilots Association—met to talk over the ideal requirements for a civil aircraft. They hammered out ideas for creating more space on the flight deck, for providing a foolproof lay-out of instruments and how the controls could be easily seen and reached by captain and first officer.

Mr Masefield, when chief executive, had called the Vanguard BEA's 'great white hope'. The airline was once again working side by side with Vickers and Rolls-Royce. They looked at 60 designs which incorporated every combination of principles: 50 to 130 seats; high-mounted wings, wings in the middle of the fuselage; large circular bodies and 'double-bubble' constructions.

BEA wanted the plane to have 90–100 seats, a cruising speed of 425 mph, Viscount-type windows and the double layer fuselage in which passengers were seated on top and a huge amount of freight could be stowed in the lower half. A host of other detailed maintenance, servicing and handling points were agreed upon after BEA's demands had been submitted. The Specification of Requirements issued by the airline ran to 50 pages. The first order was for six of the V.951 design and 14 of the later V.953s. There was no turning back and no-one wanted to. This was the Viscount's successor, potentially the best plane in the world. When it emerged it was about the same size and speed of the Bristol Britannia which BOAC operated. But the Vanguard had been specially designed for short trips and was likely to be more economic for BEA.

The first Vanguard flew in April 1959 and BEA had the first of its 20 in operation little more than 18 months later. Trans-Canada Air Lines (now Air Canada) had followed BEA by ordering the Viscount and in doing so opened up a vast market for it in North America. Now TCA took the first of its 23 Vanguards.

But the pipe dream ended there. America had produced its own turbo-props by this time. Jets had arrived and BEA itself had introduced the Comet 4. The turbo-prop's short hour of glory had gone, most of it taken by the Viscount, which was still enjoying a huge success. Had the Vanguard been so tailor-made that it would fit only BEA? It was a popular argument. Was it engine troubles as the plane was about to go into service that put off other airlines? Whatever the truth, the Vanguard never advanced beyond those first two orders.

The symbol of the flying key and a motto 'Clavis Europae' (the Key to Europe) still held good when BEA approached Moscow in 1958, its first real peep behind the Iron Curtain. Unlocking the door to Eastern Europe was not easy. Lord Douglas made a six-day visit to Moscow in February 1958 and signed an agreement with Russia's one airline, Aeroflot, to begin flights between the Soviet capital and London. This 'significant development in East–West relations' had come after years of delicate negotiations. There was no way of telling how long the arrangement might last or what might break such a fragile link.

BEA had once again blazed a trail, but it almost went wrong when new maps for passengers were slipped into the pockets of the seats. Poland protested strongly about the way its frontier with Germany and the Oder–Neisse territories were listed. The old maps had shown them as being 'under Polish administration', a phrase taken from the Potsdam Treaty which had given the area to Poland. It had been omitted on the new maps, a move taken by BEA after consultation with the Foreign Office. A spokesman for the airline in Warsaw said the new map would be more in line with reality. His counterpart in Germany said he would go on using the old ones, but pointed out that they were of no political significance and only a service to passengers. Such a 'diplomatic incident' could have been construed as an insult to the Communist powers, but fortunately for BEA the Russians chose to ignore it.

The Moscow–London route would bring in a small revenue, and prestige played a large part in its justification. BEA director Lord Balfour of Inchrye hit back against the criticisms while the proving flight was being staged and said, 'If BEA's sole consideration for starting every new route was immediate economic self-balancing, it is very doubtful that new routes would be started at all.'

Flights to Moscow began in May 1959 and Mr Khruschev did not object. BEA's chief worries were that the runways be kept clear of snow and that alternative airports were available in the emergencies a Russian winter might create.

The Number One route continued to be London–Paris which the Viscount was covering in 65 minutes. It is unlikely that this bridge over the channel will ever cease to be the busiest international air route in the world. When the *Daily Mail* set out to celebrate 50 years of flying between France and Britain in 1959 some of BEA's employees decided to join in.

The celebration took the form of a race between Marble Arch and the Arc de Triomphe, a tribute to Bleriot's first Channel crossing in 1909. BEA would make no official contribution, but with the same spirit that had prompted the Viscount team in the New Zealand Air Race six years earlier, 13 senior BEA executives with bowler hats, briefcases and umbrellas hired a London bus and scrambled into diesel trains, a Comet and a fleet of French taxis to complete the course in 61 minutes. Their efforts won them a £1,000 team prize. The individual winner of the race staggered everyone by recording a time of 40 minutes 44 seconds.

This little piece of midsummer madness coincided with BEA carrying its twenty millionth passenger. There were now 100,000 passengers a week travelling BEA. As if to acknowledge the sporting spirit of the Air Race, BEA

bought up a 30-acre site near Northolt for use as a sports ground. After 13 years of away fixtures the cricket, soccer, tennis, bowls and netball teams could play at home.

BEA had a large stake in the new College of Air Training at Hamble in Hampshire which was opened in May 1960. But the chairman shunned the opening ceremony to attend the beginning of the British Trade Fair in Moscow. BEA had taken 600 square feet of space and Lord Douglas's role was ambassador for Britain as well as representative for the airline. The Russians were concerned over the amount of traffic BEA was getting on the new air route between capitals and in order to keep its rights to fly to Moscow, BEA signed a pool agreement which meant it would share takings on the sector with Aeroflot. The agreement eliminated any element of competition on the route.

The biggest profit ever, over two million pounds, was recorded in 1960, but BEA were not going to throw it away. Pilots were asked to take it easy while taxiing around the airports. Wear-and-tear on brakes and tyres was costing too much. Punctuality, however desirable, must not be achieved by high-speed 'motoring' between flights.

Ever anxious for more passengers, the corporation introduced the world's lowest air fare of £3 3s (£3·15) on the London to Glasgow and Edinburgh flights. It worked out at about $2\frac{1}{4}$d (1p) a mile. None of the tourist fares, special rates for excursions or off-peak journeys anywhere in the world over a similar distance could compete with it. Then an agreement was signed with Air France which, it was hoped, would cut fares between Britain and France by 15–20 per cent. Lord Douglas speculated that the two airlines might get as many as 50 per cent more passengers through the agreement. Once again, the pact would make life easier for travellers, but the needle of competition was blunted.

There was no shortage of ideas in BEA, even when it came to publicity stunts. A quartet of mop-haired young-

How Ringo Starr of the Beatles helped the BEA publicity drive

sters had fought their way to the top of the hit parade in 1964 and public relations officer Harry Berry was determined to do something about the obvious link between BEA and the BEAtles. The group was about to fly BEA when Mr Berry hit upon his idea. Get a piece of hardboard painted up with the letters 'TLES' and hope that the boys will agree to hold it next to a BEA sign when they board their aircraft.

But it was not as simple as that. The sign was made to fit the letters on a Vanguard, the plane in which the Beatles were travelling. At the last minute the group changed its booking and switched to a Comet. John, Paul and George struggled through the screaming fans at Heathrow airport, London, to board their plane. But Ringo had been stranded in Liverpool by fog and came through London the next day. There were no crowd problems and Ringo was happy to oblige by posing with the 'TLES' sign on the steps of a Vanguard before boarding his Paris-bound Comet.

Other airlines were green with envy over the publicity BEA got in the national newspapers. Nor were the competitors any happier when the group returned. More pictures were taken, this time of the four stars carrying BEA overnight bags with 'The' and 'TLES' printed on either side of the airline's square red badge.

Beatlemania was at its height, but BEA was more con-

Look, no hands! A convincing demonstration of the automatic landing gear on a Trident

cerned with a scheme which would beat the delays caused by fog. The implications of an automatic landing system are of the utmost importance. Weather conditions change rapidly so does visibility. More than ten full working days were lost at Heathrow airport in the winter of 1958/59 because of fogs. BEA lost £250,000 as a result.

In October 1965, a BEA Vanguard was attempting to land at Heathrow in fog with visibility hovering on the safety margin. At the last moment, the captain decided to overshoot. But it was too late and the plane crashed, killing 29 passengers and seven crew. Several years later an Afghan Airlines Boeing 727 crashed on an approach to Gatwick airport in foggy conditions. These accidents might never have happened if the weather had been clear, or if the planes had been equipped with automatic landing systems.

The first crude attempt at landing an aircraft automatically had been made in 1948. The purpose of such experiments was to beat the weather and eliminate the need for a pilot to rely on his eyesight when landing his plane. Delays and diversions in foggy weather cost BEA and others millions of pounds a year. Supersonic airliners such as Concorde need automatic landing equipment if their passengers are to be given the full benefit of travelling at twice the speed of sound. There is little point in dashing across the Atlantic in 3½ hours if hours more are wasted in circling a fogbound airport.

Experiments to disperse fog with chemical sprays or by burning flares have been unsuccessful and far too costly. BEA decided to introduce an automatic 'blind landing' system when the first of its Trident jets came along. The British-designed 'Autoland' system fitted into the new jets had three automatic pilots. If one failed the other would override the fault and the aircraft could continue on the course which had been programmed into the equipment.

Pilots could keep their hands off the controls until after the aircraft had landed, but were instructed to keep them on in case of emergency. Captains and first officers were still required to monitor landings but there was no need to touch a single switch. Trials began as soon as the Trident was delivered. It was to be a slow and much-practised procedure. Every step was carefully examined. The first 'blind' landings were made in clear weather at remote airfields by planes carrying a minimum of crew and no

A Trident using autoland in heavy fog

passengers. Experience of automatic landings built up—the most noticeable difference to a layman is the repeated change in the whine of the jets as the throttles are 'see-sawed' up and down by the Autoland system.

The pilot had to set the speed required, select the appropriate radio channels, programme the essential information into the system and then sit back. The rate of descent, speed, throttle settings and attitude of the plane were adjusted automatically as touchdown was neared. The controlling authority in Britain demanded that automatic landing systems in passenger-carrying planes had a safety factor of less than one failure in ten million.

The world's first automatic landing by a passenger-carrying jet was made on 10th June 1965—a bright summer's day. Eighty passengers on BEA's Paris to London flight BE 343 hardly noticed the difference. More than 600 trial landings had been made previously. The pilot knew that if he was not satisfied with the aircraft's approach he could switch in a second to manual control, or instantly programme the system to overshoot and 'go round again'. Little by little, the airline has crept up to the point where perfect landings can be achieved in poor visibility.

BEA was granted the Queen's Award to Industry for technological achievement in automatic landings in 1970. Planes could not be landed in thick fogs or other conditions where visibility was nil, but a number of significant steps had been taken towards that goal.

CHAPTER 4

THE JETS ARE COMING

No OTHER single invention has had such a dramatic effect on flying as the jet engine. Jet airliners climb high into the rarefied air over the clouds, leaving behind every kind of adverse weather. They fly 200 mph faster than piston-engined or turbo-prop aircraft and are cheaper to run. Jet engines have far fewer moving parts; they are more reliable and need less maintenance. Every new invention has its snags. But the gremlins had been driven out of the jet engine by 20 years experience with military aircraft by the time planemakers began mass producing jet planes for the airlines. The jets brought a new way of life for pilots, stewardesses and passengers. Timetables had to be completely re-written. Flying techniques were totally different. Leisurely lunches gave way to quick cups of tea as the new planes hurtled across the world six, seven or eight miles high.

The most dramatic changes came in intercontinental flights. Jets had time to reach a high cruising altitude, where flying was more comfortable and cheaper, before levelling off to cross oceans. But on BEA's journeys of a few hundred miles there was hardly time to reach the best height. Operated at a few thousand feet, jets cost more to run than propeller planes. Understandably, BEA was not among the first to fly jets.

The Comets which crashed in 1954 gave a false start to jet flying. While British engineers were solving the Comet's problems, the French were developing the twin-engined short range Caravelle. The jet from France was to match the Viscount in popularity and well over 250 were sold. The key to its success was the revolutionary idea of placing the engines right at the back. This left the wings uncluttered so that flaps, ailerons and air brakes could be kept simple and create the maximum effect. The engines were easy to reach for maintenance and replacement and much of the noise was eliminated from the passenger cabin.

Every major airline in Europe apart from BEA, KLM and Lufthansa ordered Caravelles. BEA stuck with the British aircraft industry and worked out a short-haul version of the Comet—the 4B. In March 1958 BEA ordered six and was happy to find its faith in the British industry justified. The Comet was introduced in April 1960 and made a handsome profit. The 4B could cruise at 550 mph and carried up to a hundred people.

There were times, however, when jet-age travel was not as glamorous as it might have been. Comedienne Dora Bryan was less than cheerful when she wrote to BEA about her flight back from a holiday in Spain. She was to have flown home from Gibraltar. But an electrical storm prevented the Comet landing and after a 30-hour delay, Miss Bryan and 85 other passengers were driven 150 miles

Left: Heathrow at night, from beneath the wing of a Comet

in a coach to Seville where the plane had been diverted. The weary travellers boarded the plane and then it happened. Said Miss Bryan:

'I know it sounds fantastic, but we were told the battery had run flat. I ask you, the battery running flat on a Comet! It took them 15 hours to recharge it. Eventually, we arrived at London airport at 2 a.m. on Thursday instead of in the early hours of Tuesday. It really is too much. We were 40 hours late.'

The unhappy staff in London could only apologise and offer the irate comedienne a free ride home by car from the airport. Seville was not normally used by BEA and there had been no ground apparatus there to start the Comet's engines. The plane had landed to await a break in the weather at Gibraltar, but none came. This delay and the wait for the passengers to arrive in the coach resulted in the aircraft standing idle for 24 hours—long enough for the batteries to run down.

BEA's second jet, the Trident, took eight years to emerge. It had its beginnings in the autumn of 1956 when four firms submitted designs for an aircraft tailored to BEA's needs. The final choice for the £30 million order rested between de Havilland's Project 121 and the Bristol 200. There were political reasons favouring first one aircraft, then the other. BEA made up its mind in August 1957 that it would choose the DH121, but it had to wait for Government blessing before making the announcements. Press and public were kept guessing for six months. Hawker Siddeley had sided with the Bristol project, but long after the issue was decided they took over the firm of de Havillands and the DH121 is known today as the Hawker Siddeley Trident.

Seldom had there been such angry scenes and arguments over the choosing of a design. Newspapers reported 'civil war' between aircraft workers, of squabbles in the House of Commons and feuds in the aircraft industry. Sir Miles Thomas, chairman of BOAC, wrote to the *Daily Telegraph* and thundered that the biggest danger was a delay in the decision. Sir Thomas Sopwith, chairman of Hawker Siddeley, rejected claims that the Bristol 200 was inferior. But de Havillands said nothing. They had been told that if the airline was allowed to decide, it would choose their design and the team which had built the Comet.

The new plane promised to combine the best features of every known civil aircraft. It would have three jet engines at the rear, swept-back wings, a large passenger cabin, a speed of 600 mph and a range of 1,000 miles. There were high hopes that large export orders would follow. It was, after all, being built with the Government's blessing and it was to be flown by a famous nationalised airline.

In the meantime, it was necessary for pilots and ground staffs in BEA to learn all there was to know about flying jets. Planes with propellers take-off at slower speeds and climb undramatically. Aerial manoeuvres and landings would now have to be precise operations. To take-off in a jet, the throttles are opened to full power and the plane leaps forward when the brakes are released. It races over the tarmac, pressing passengers back in their seats. Nearly 100 tons of metal hurtle down a two-mile runway reaching 180 mph in 30 seconds. Halfway along, it lifts into the air and climbs away at a steep angle. No earlier form of power could have achieved such a spectacular take-off.

In minutes the plane reaches its cruising altitude seven miles up and levels off. Clouds, storms, rain and snow are left far below. Up high it is safer, smoother, cheaper—and every day is a sunny one. Navigation must be quick and accurate. The distance between London and Paris could be covered in 20 minutes by a 600 mph Trident.

Some pilots, when asked to transfer to this new form of air travel, found it too big a change. The habits formed in a lifetime of flying planes with propellers could not be adapted over night. A few pilots were afraid and looked upon the new aircraft as spaceships rather than aeroplanes. Others found going back to school in middle age beyond them. All pilots are given thorough medical checks every six months and are regularly tested to see that they have kept up with the latest skills and drills. The ordinary process of keeping up to scratch was enough for some, without having to think of learning new procedures. It was a burden to have the lives of 50 passengers strapped to one's back, let alone 150.

Jet pilots had to learn how to put on an oxygen mask in a hurry and bring a plane down six miles without upsetting passengers or snapping the wings. These emergency drills had to be practised although they were probably never going to be used. Captains and first officers had to learn that to stay ahead of the aircraft in their thinking, throttles had to be pulled back long before destinations came in sight. The sleek lines of the jet produce very little drag and levelling off from a climb could bring about a sudden, dramatic and unwanted acceleration.

Undercarriages, flaps and speed brakes have to be extended to produce drag artificially—it is not enough to just pull off the power.

Proper use of fuel had to be discovered, too. A pilot in a piston-engined plane looks for a landing field if he is low on fuel. A jet pilot climbs as high as he can where his plane will use fuel at a minimum rate. Altitude provides range and allows the pilot a wider choice of airfields—he can throttle back and power-glide to the one which suits him best.

The jet pilot has also to realise that swept-back wings made planes less stable, that the nose of his aircraft must be kept high at low speeds and that jet engines work best at high speeds and in cold climates. Tipping the plane back on its tail restricts the amount of air entering the engine intakes, so jets must be kept running fast when approaching a landing. Flaps, air brakes and the wheels are stuck out to regulate the speed and with everything 'out and down', the jet lands like a galleon under full sail. In this way the aircraft is controllable and safe.

Modern technology has made jets easy to fly and light on the controls. The wings, tail and engine do not ice-up so much. There are fewer instruments to watch, fewer switches and levers. All these points were being learned by BEA's new breed of pilots while the DH121 was being built. It first flew in January 1962 and was named Trident. BEA had abandoned individual christenings—the fact that it was a jet gave it sufficient appeal.

The Trident bristled with new equipment. It had three engines and everything else seemed to be in triplicate. Each control had three systems to operate it; a failure of two was considered highly unlikely and three would be just about impossible. Warning lights on the flight deck lit up in triplicate so that any malfunction—shown by a flashing red or amber light—could be spotted by the pilot, first officer or engineer. The passengers were attended by three stewards, naturally.

The three engines clustered round the tail allowed much larger safety margins. The chances of a jet engine failing are a million to one against. But if it did happen, even at take-off or while cruising, the aircraft could continue its journey in complete safety. Better still, the aircraft did not have to sit waiting at a foreign airfield for spares to be flown in—it could take-off empty on two engines and, if necessary, land with just one working. The days when BEA had a special freighter to carry spare engines to stranded planes had long since past.

The Trident was designed with its own auxiliary power unit for starting the engines; keeping lighting, heating and other electrical systems going when on the ground. There would be no flat batteries here! Engineers had recognised from the start that BEA wanted to be able to service its planes overnight and everything possible was done to allow this. Refuelling was not necessary at all BEA's destinations because of the short distances and even when it was, a full load could be taken on by a Trident in eleven minutes.

Every detail was carefully thought out. The nosewheel was fitted slightly to one side under the fuselage, rather than the conventional middle position, to allow a saving in weight and fractionally more space in the baggage hold.

The aircraft had to be different because BEA's work

was, and is, different. The Trident was faster than any other commercial jet, but it could be flown at a profit on the shortest of routes, those which bring in the lowest amount of money. It was built to combat the threat of Air France's Caravelle, and like its rival it had engines at the rear. But the Trident was of such a design that there was room for enlargements. The fuselage could be 'stretched' to allow for more seats and the engines could be made more powerful. BEA's chairman, Lord Douglas, began talking of further orders even before the first Trident went into service.

The first fare-paying passengers to fly in the new plane did so by chance. They were to have gone by Comet from London to Copenhagen in March 1964, but there was room to spare on the first Trident which was taking pressmen and a BBC television crew. It was the maiden voyage of the first three-engined jet in the world. The tailor-made plane had begun work on time.

With the jets came soaring figures for all sections of the airline's operation. The 25 million passengers mark had been passed in 1960. Three years later a surprised commercial manager on his way from Scotland to London was plied with champagne, presents and a free ticket to celebrate his being the 40 millionth passenger. On 23rd July 1965, the wife of a British Army officer found herself being presented with a 50-guinea cheque for being the 50 millionth. The first 25 million came in 14 years and the second 25 million in less than five.

The arrival of the jets pushed the Viscount on to the less glamorous domestic routes. In time, jets would also oust the much-publicised Vanguard and relegate it to a cargo-carrying role. Freighting was the quiet side of BEA which seldom received publicity, but nevertheless earned a substantial income. The airline had used one Bristol freighter in the fifties, mainly for carrying spares and replacement engines to stranded Elizabethans. Now the increase in freight and mail forced BEA to buy special cargo carriers.

The Argosy is the easiest aircraft of all to recognise. It has four engines and a bulbous hold which stops short of the high, twin tail fins. Two slim struts project back from the inboard engines and are joined by a plank-like tailwing connecting the fins. To those accustomed to the basic shapes of passenger planes, the Argosy looked like a designer's nightmare.

BEA's air freight included fish, birds, monkeys, snakes, crocodiles, lizards, cats and dogs. Occasionally it might involve a lion, a tiger, or an elephant. It was BEA's sad duty to bring back the giant Panda, Chi Chi, from Russia after an unsuccessful courtship with An An. Unusual cargoes had to be expected in the ever-increasing volume BEA handled.

Dozens of racehorses were flown to stud farms or important race meetings. Racing cars had to be transported for international events all over Europe. If an orchestra went on tour there would be hundreds of music instruments to be flown out with it.

Not just people but everything from dogs to Chi-Chi the reluctant Panda fly BEA

BEA has also carried huge amounts of mail. There have been few years when figures for tons of freight and mail on international and domestic services have not risen, as the following tables show:

YEAR	FREIGHT	MAIL	YEAR	FREIGHT	MAIL
1947	668	510	1959	28,020	7,669
1948	2,610	1,558	1960	36,395	7,848
1949	4,426	2,981	1961	41,996	8,850
1950	6,093	4,168	1962	41,042	9,325
1951	10,079	5,249	1963	49,290	12,115
1952	12,500	6,489	1964	58,259	12,997
1953	14,328	6,289	1965	72,561	14,089
1954	14,559	6,582	1966	92,362	15,100
1955	14,884	6,964	1967	110,021	16,430
1956	18,586	7,895	1968	115,932	14,791
1957	22,524	7,541	1969	132,422	15,581
1958	24,555	7,465	1970	130,758	16,436

Shetland Islanders from North Ronaldsay, flower growers in the Scilly Islands and market gardeners in the Channel Islands saw the potential of fast air freight services in the forties. Perishable goods including foodstuffs, plant life and even newspapers went by BEA from the start. Then the jet age cut time in transit to the minimum.

There are some things that jets cannot alter, however. One is the time spent getting to and from airports. On the London–Paris route the total time between city centres has been reduced by less than an hour in 40 years. The pre-war biplanes took well over two hours in the air and today's jets take less than one hour. But BEA's red buses, towing their baggage trailers along the M4 motorway to Heathrow, are too often to be seen in the thickest of London's traffic jams. The London–Paris air race showed that it was possible to complete the journey in 41 minutes. Twelve years later it still takes the ordinary passenger a minimum of 2½ hours.

One of the biggest headaches with jets has been the problem of noise. In 1960 BEA restricted Comet flights at night to taking-off in only three of the twelve directions then available at London airport. The practice of running up the engines to full power against the brakes was abandoned and jet pilots were instructed to make rolling starts from taxiways. At 3,000 feet they throttled back to keep noise levels on the ground as low as possible.

A vintage Rolls flown in by BEA freight from West Germany

Mail for Belfast being loaded automatically onto a Viscount

66

The level of noise depends on atmospherics and the weight of the aircraft. Noise restrictions sometimes forced aircraft to make additional stops in the middle of long journeys to take on fuel. Jet engines are now fitted with noise suppressors or have modifications to make them quieter. Very occasionally, it is impossible for noise limits and safety margins to be observed simultaneously.

Jet aircraft cost millions of pounds each. When flying first began, an inexperienced pilot could put his foot through a wing and be faced with a bill of under £10. But an elementary error (although you cannot stamp a hole in the wings!) with a jet can be enormously expensive, as BEA found out soon after the first short haul jets appeared at London airport. One of the airline's electricians, linking up a ground power unit to the fuselage of a jet to start the engines, connected it incorrectly. In seconds serious damage had been inflicted on the plane's electrical system. Repairs cost £30,000 and the aircraft was grounded for six days.

The shortage of pilots in the fifties gave BEA a unique opportunity. Radio-telephone links and other modern means of communication between aircraft and the ground had made BEA's 176 radio operators redundant. Many of them were delighted to accept a new challenge and start training as pilots. In the past, the corporations had insisted that recruits for flying duties had a commercial pilot's licence. The radio operators were halfway towards this qualification, being familiar with the controls and techniques of modern aircraft. If anything, they were better than recruits with the ink on their licences still wet.

Training was costly. Aeroplanes could not earn money while engaged in training flights and inevitably some of them were damaged by heavy landings or taxiing accidents. New pilots found themselves making their first 'flights' without ever leaving the ground. Their first touches of the controls came in a simulator, an exact replica of the control cabin or flight deck of an aircraft. A flying simulator contains everything that is to be found on a

A Viscount's speciality: the baby hammock

63

This Trident 'Papa Sierra' was gutted by fire on the ground in 1969.
The arsonist was never caught. Here workmen do a ruthless job of
dismantling the aircraft before it makes its last journey to the scrapyard

real plane and the cabin is made to the same scale. The crew take up the places in the usual way with the captain in the left-hand seat and the co-pilot on his right. All modern aircraft have duplicated controls and can be flown from either position. But the captain or pilot in command always sits in the left-hand seat.

The simulator is equipped with all the controls and instruments of a real aircraft. Engine and other noises peculiar to the type of plane are relayed and they are varied with the simulated speed to achieve realism. The pilot is made to feel pressures and gusts of wind which would be experienced normally when handling the controls. Sometimes the windows are merely blacked out, but often a television picture of a runway is projected in the window area. Take-offs, landings, navigating and flying in cloud can be simulated. All actions by the pilot on the controls are transmitted to a computer and the simulator reacts accordingly. The instruments tell the same story as they would in actual flight.

Instructors stand outside the 'aircraft' in the room which houses the equipment. They can feed engine or under-carriage failures into the flight and test pilots' reactions to any kind of emergency. Navigational problems, fuel shortages, fog clampdowns, engine fires or faulty warning lights or instruments can confront the trainee. But no matter what action is taken, the pilot and his dummy plane cannot be hurt by a 'crash'.

Simulators cost tens of thousands of pounds and can be used for hundreds of 'flights' a year. But each new type of plane needs a new simulator and there are always pilots waiting to take a six-monthly check test or to be trained on a new type. Getting airborne on the ground can save the airline a lot of money, providing it has recruits with a sound knowledge and experience of the air.

The simulator for BEA's Comets arrived before the first of the new aircraft in 1959. It was in action almost nonstop for the first five months as propeller-trained pilots converted to the new technique. Hundreds of pilots were also converting to Viscounts, for which there were two simulators. A new one was being built for Vanguards.

When the abolition of National Service stemmed the flow of ex-service pilots, BEA joined with BOAC and the Ministry of Aviation to set up a College of Air Training at Hamble, Hampshire. It was to take young men between the ages of 18 and 24 who were sponsored by the airlines. They were given a comprehensive course of basic and advanced flying, geared to the requirements of becoming airline pilots.

It was important that pilots did not arrive at BEA and BOAC for training in large and expensive aircraft such as jets with bad habits and slack thinking on safety procedures which could have worked into their flying. The corporations wanted the best recruits and the most skilful pilots, but they did not want careless fliers, or dare-devils who ignored safety checks. Prince Philip opened the college in May 1961 and the first cadets arrived for training four months later. An immediate shortage was overcome when BEA sent a selection board to Canada which recruited 30 pilots from Trans-Canada Airlines and the Royal Canadian Air Force.

The first graduates left Hamble in 1962 and those who joined BEA were soon flying the big jets at Stansted, Essex, or at other airfields commonly used for training flights. But the English climate intervened all too frequently and prompted BEA to do something about the costly delays in flying training. Aircraft, instructors, pupils and mechanics were transferred to Malta. For the first time civil pilots were being trained outside Britain.

Not only did courses take two months less in the continuously clear conditions, but £20,000 was saved. In the first month only eight hours, or just over three per cent, of training time was lost. Strong cross-winds were the only conditions which prevented flying. At Stansted the figure would have been 67 per cent. Landing fees of more than £16,000 were paid to the Maltese and 5,000 gallons of fuel a day had to be bought. But it was still cheaper than

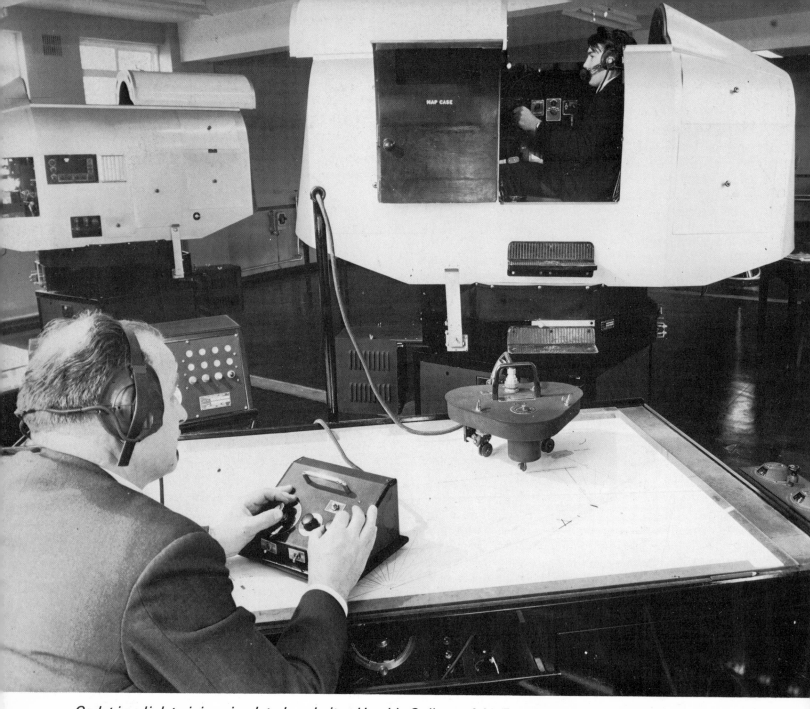

70 *Cadet in a link training simulated cockpit at Hamble College of Air Training*

Class in session at Hamble College of Air Training

having training flights grounded at home in Britain.

The college at Hamble continues to train future BEA pilots. In the first ten years it sent 367 to BEA and another 252 to BOAC. Training is carried out with Piper Cherokees, de Havilland Chipmunks and Beechcraft Barons. In its busiest year, the college's planes flew 32,000 hours and logged more than 100,000 take-offs and landings.

The increasing volume of air traffic over the area restricted expansion and other schools are now used. One is at Kidlington airport, Oxford, six miles outside the city. It is too small for jets or commercial aircraft, but the light planes run by the flying school and by private clubs make

the airport one of the busiest in the country. It copes with 132,000 take-offs and landings a year.

Oxford now contributes more than £1 million a year to Britain's invisible exports by teaching basic training to future airport pilots from countries in Europe, Africa and even Japan. A third source of new pilots is the school at Perth. Just like those at Hamble and Oxford, the Scottish base is a few miles from the centre of an ancient city. The youngsters begin their jet-age careers with simple circuits giving them the most exhilarating views out over Southampton Water, around Blenheim Palace, or high over the River Tay and Scotland's former capital city.

A row of gleaming Tridents, bright as guardsmen's boots

CHAPTER 5

SHOWING THE FLAG

FOR AN AIRLINE which boasted of buying British to the exclusion of all other types of aircraft, BEA got a lot of mileage out of the American DC-3 Dakota. The claim is valid, however, because BEA never bought new DC-3s. It was given a lot of them when it left BOAC behind and first went solo, and it acquired a good few at second-hand as the years went by.

The record of this remarkable plane is without parallel. Some 13,000 Dakotas were built, thousands more than any other kind of transport aircraft. The majority came from the United States but hundreds were built under licence in other countries. Collectively, they are estimated to have carried some 750 million passengers in 36 years. About 500 were still flying with civil and military air forces around the world in 1970.

The first DC-3 sold for £20,350 in the thirties and after the war the price rose to £35,700. The plane was slow, unpressurised and cumbersome to manoeuvre. But it was a solid flier. Hundreds of heroic deeds were attributed to Dakota pilots and the majority of them were helped by the airworthiness of the plane. One pilot flew 40 miles and landed safely after his port wing struck the side of a mountain and a section twelve feet long was ripped off.

The jet age was the final blow for BEA's fleet of DC-3s. Over a period of 16 years they served the airline in every way possible. Their brief hour of glory for BEA began when they were the only aircraft the corporation possessed.

Then the Viking appeared and the 'Dak' was relegated to a supporting role. Viscounts and Elizabethans pushed it out of international service all together. Yet it was still the cheapest plane to run over journeys of up to 410 miles. Finally, after seven years on domestic duties, it had sunk to bottom place in the profit-making league table and retirement came with a flight from Islay via Campbeltown to Glasgow in May 1962.

BEA flew the old workhorse to every major city in Europe. It underwent major surgery to become the Pionair, a slightly larger and more comfortable version. It carried freight as the Pionair/Leopard. It acted as a flying testbed for the Dart engine and was something of a super-freighter as the Dart-Dakota. Having served on local services there was nothing left; no other way could be found to make use of it. One pilot summed up BEA's feeling for the DC-3 when he said:

'We cursed it, we kicked and chivvied it, but it was like a pack mule just plodding along and never letting you down.'

At one stage, BEA had as many as 50 in its fleet. A total of 58 were used by the airline and they flew 97 million miles carrying $8\frac{1}{2}$ million passengers. The last batch of six was sold off and continued flying for several years with independent airlines.

Manufacturers tried to cash in and build a replacement for the DC-3. Early attempts failed because the replacements cost more to run than the original. Later ones could not be adapted to cover the vast range of missions the old aircraft was capable of carrying out. Starting as a 14-passenger sleeper transport equipped with bunk beds, the DC-3 became famous in 1936 in its 21-seat version. BEA's Pionairs carried 32 passengers and other modifications enlarged the cabin to accommodate 36, more than 2½ times the number the original plane had been designed to take. The second world war sent production figures rocketing; over 10,000 were built for American and allied air forces and airlines. Only 803 were completed in the post-war years, but many of the wartime models were converted for civil use. The DC-3 cruised at 170 mph, almost the speed at which Tridents take off!

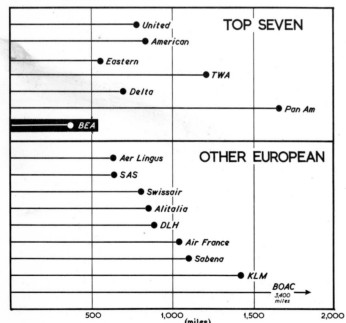

A chart showing average passenger journey length in miles during 1968. At less than 500 miles, BEA stands out as the 'shorthaul' specialist

Its retirement coincided with that of BEA's Viscount 701s, the first mass-produced version of the world-famous airliner. While the DC-3 had been the world's most widely used transport plane, the Viscount was Britain's best-selling passenger aircraft. BEA bought 27 V.701s which carried six million passengers. But when they were sold the airline still had 39 of the later versions.

Soon after these departures, Lord Douglas of Kirtleside, chairman and father-figure to BEA, decided to retire. (*See Chapter* 9.) His arrival had had a profound effect on the fortunes of the airline. But while his departure after 15 years was a sad occasion, it was obvious that BEA had grown up and needed a new kind of leadership.

No other chairman of a nationalised concern before or since has served continuously for so long. Lord Douglas's going coincided with the announcement of a record profit for BEA—over £3 million for the first time. It was as if his successor, Sir Anthony Milward and the staff of 17,000 had timed it deliberately as a tribute and a parting gift to their popular chief.

There was now an entirely new look about the airline, but some changes seemed to come too fast. One which was to send pulse rates soaring was that by Dutch-born Rinske Hali, an 18-year-old blonde model, in a bikini. Blue-eyed Rinske was hired in December 1964 by a BEA photographer who had been assigned to take pictures of beach scenes at Sitges, Spain, for posters and advertisements. Rinske had not brought her own bikini and had to borrow one. The results were sensational and advertisements for BEA featuring Rinske appeared in the national newspapers. But an MP and others saw it as an outrage to BEA's image. Strong objections were voiced. Rinske was bewildered, but slightly amused by the fuss. Two years later, 40 girls in bikinis lined up for judges to choose which one would appear in a BEA advertisement. The occasion passed without the raising of a solitary eyebrow.

The bikini row was not the first time that MPs and the public had tried jealously to guard what they thought the airline's image should be. BEA had made a success in Europe of 'being British' and it was closely identified with the British way of life. In these circumstances, some observers found any departure from the patriotic past, any 'cheapening' of BEA's image, or lowering of the national flag hard to tolerate.

In 1951, it had been considered a crime when the initials B.E.A. were written across the corporation's coat of arms. An official of the college of Arms exclaimed that it was a 'stupid and ridiculous thing to do' as the coat of arms should act as an identification in itself. Once, it was pointed out, the Earl Marshal's Court meted out severe and terrible punishments to deal with such infringements, but chief executive Mr Peter Masefield was not impressed.

'We shall do nothing about it. This is a commercial world,' he said.

Despite a strictly business approach, BEA has always followed a policy of supporting the British aircraft industry wherever possible. Even when just one or two planes of a particular type were needed, they were always taken from the home market. BEA had supported the four-engined de Havilland Heron when it emerged in the fifties and two of these small planes are still operating its air ambulance service in Scotland.

The airline also backed the Handley Page Herald, a 56-seat twin-engined airliner capable of 275 mph. The Herald arrived in the early sixties. It could not have had a better advertisement than that given it by Prince Philip's tour of South America in 1962. Two Heralds, one owned by BEA, were used for an aerial tour of eleven countries and were frequently flown by the royal pilot. Both planes were fitted with long-range fuel tanks and high frequency radios. Flight and cabin crews were provided by BEA. Prince Philip said after visiting 38 airfields and covering more than 20,000 miles, 'The two Heralds gave excellent service throughout my tour.'

BEA's initial order for Trident Ones was backed up with the purchase of 15 Trident Twos. They could carry up to 40 more passengers but BEA operates them at a maximum of 97 seats—three more than the Trident One's capacity. The thrust of the engines had been increased. The wingspan was an extra eight feet but the new jets were fractionally faster than the first batch. In time, this order was to be followed by one of 26 for the Trident Three. The huge re-equipment policy was completed when 18 BAC One-Elevens were bought, mainly for use on BEA's internal German network. (*See Chapter* 6.)

This table shows the different types of passenger and freight-carrying aircraft, excluding helicopters, used by BEA in its first 25 years.

AIRCRAFT	ALTERNATIVE NAMES	NUMBER ACQUIRED
Douglas DC-3 Dakota	Pionair, Pionair/Leopard, Dart-Dakota	58
Avro 19	XIX	12
Junkers Ju 52/3m	Jupiter	11
De Havilland DH89 Dragon Rapide	Dominie, Islander	45
Vickers Viking 1A	—	22
Vickers Viking 1B	Admiral	53
Airspeed AS.57 Ambassador	Elizabethan	20
Bristol Freighter 21	—	1
Vickers Viscount V.630	—	1
Vickers Viscount V.701	Discovery	27
Vickers Viscount V.732, V. 736, V.745 and V.779	—	7*
Vickers Viscount V.802	Discovery	24
Vickers Viscount V.806	Discovery	20
De Havilland Heron 1B	Hebrides	5
Handley Page Herald	—	3
Vickers Vanguard 951	—	6
Vickers Vanguard 953	Merchantman	14
Armstrong Whitworth Argosy 102	—	3
Armstrong Whitworth Argosy 222	—	6
De Havilland Comet 4B	—	18
Hawker Siddeley Trident 1C	DH.121	23
Hawker Siddeley Trident 2E	—	15
BAC One-Eleven 510-ED	Super One-Eleven	18
Hawker Siddeley Trident 3B	—	26†

* One V.732 and two each of the others.
† First delivered spring, 1971. Most still on order.

In addition, one or more of the following types have been used by BEA or associated companies for communications, research or other activities: Avro Anson, Auster, DH84 Dragon 2, DH60G Moth, Mercury M.28, Mosquito.

One Avro Lancaster and five Lancastrian IIIs were registered to BEA but not used by the airline. Also excluded are a number of aircraft, mainly prototypes, which were painted in BEA's colours but not owned by the airline nor operated by it on passenger or freight carrying flights. (*For helicopters see Chapter* 10.)

Most of the Dakotas, Avro 19s, Jupiters, and Dragon Rapides were inherited, acquired by, or 'wished on' to BEA soon after it was formed. All the three hundred or so planes BEA has ever bought have been British. Spread over 25 years, it has purchased an average of more than one a month. The total amount spent on aircraft is well over £300 million.

The airline has consistently bought British equipment wherever possible, but its first duty has been to its passengers and thereafter to making money for the country as a whole. There have been a number of aircraft which BEA wanted to buy, but could not do so for financial, political or other reasons. The aircraft include several foreign makes which the corporation wanted instead of the British planes it had to be content with.

When BEA introduced the Viscount, its appeal to passengers was enormous. Air France decided it could not let its British rival get away and ordered the aircraft for itself. But when the French airline was jetting ahead with the Caravelle, BEA had to buy Comets. Luckily, the Comet proved to be a winner, too.

BEA tried hard to make a success of the Fairey Rotodyne, a helicopter-cum-aeroplane. It took off and landed vertically using a rotor, and cruised horizontally when pushed by two forward-facing engines. Air travel between city centres at a price the public could afford seemed just around the corner. But the Rotodyne was too noisy, too

costly and had not been proved to enable BEA to convert its letter of intent to buy six into a firm order.

Had it been allowed a completely free hand in buying new aircraft, BEA would now be flying the 'stretched' Boeing 727 jet as Air France does on routes in Europe. A study of 16 variations of the basic design for aircraft envisaged by Boeing, Douglas, Hawker Siddeley and the British Aircraft Corporation was made in 1966 to find a jet replacement for the Vanguard. Like its competitors, BEA found the larger Boeing 727 was the most attractive. But with so few new planes on the drawing boards, an order for American equipment could have severely damaged Britain's industry. The next best buy from BEA's point of view was BAC's 211, a twin-engined type capable of carrying 190 people. But the Government refused to finance the project and BEA had to think again. Time was short and the only other aircraft available was the Trident Three.

Tridents had established themselves throughout the corporation's European network and there was no doubting their popularity with passengers. But the Trident Three was thought to be too small. Because of the decision to prevent BEA buying the aircraft of its choice, the Government had agreed that millions of pounds in compensation should be given to the corporation.

The size of an aircraft is of crucial importance. Aeroplanes make money when they can carry enough passengers paying fares which will total more than the entire cost of the journey. The sum must include booking and organisation costs, maintenance and servicing for the aircraft, depreciation and extras such as landing fees. But it is not as simple as that. Two planes carrying 60 people over a given route might not make as much money as three of a different type carrying 40 each. The effect is the same—120 people flown from one place to another—but the cost of doing so can range from totally uneconomic to highly profitable.

Sir Anthony Milward gave a lecture in 1966 in which he

said: 'The aircraft which is the ideal size for operation between London and Glasgow in mid-summer is not the ideal aircraft for London–Jersey in mid-winter, nor for Glasgow–Barra at any time. An airline cannot, however, operate aircraft of dozens of different sizes. We must compromise and operate perhaps three major types.'

Whenever size permitted, BEA has bought British. But it has gone further than that. The national flag has become BEA's trademark. A Union Jack type symbol is displayed on the tail fins of every BEA aircraft today. The symbol stands out proudly and the gleaming jets can be compared to peacocks displaying their brilliant plumages of tail feathers.

A liking for flags, symbols and being thoroughly British has brought its share of difficulties, however. British motor manufacturers protested in 1950 when BEA bought American cars for their representatives in America. Nor did it help when a spokesman said, 'The BEA board authorised the New York representative to buy an American car because it was cheaper and there was prompt delivery.'

It came as a shock, too, when the national flag was removed from the front of BEA's timetable in 1957 because 'there are places on our routes where it is slightly embarrassing'. It was replaced by the silhouette of an aircraft. People asked if BEA was ashamed of the national flag. Sir Anthony Milward, then 'Mr' and the airline's chief executive, said firmly, 'I have no apologies to make. It's purely a matter of business.' The airline had been warned by staff in Greece and the Middle East that some potential passengers might be put off by the presence of the flag. No other airline displayed a national flag on its timetable. But those who criticised BEA failed to mention that the Union Jack was still painted on the tails of the corporation's aircraft.

Newcomers to the airline in the fifties found working for BEA was often like living in a goldfish bowl. Any new move, every innovation was scrutinised by Parliament, press and public. There could be lavish praise and angry criticism from different sources heaped on the airline at the same time. But whatever the verdict, BEA was now a prominent and permanent feature of life in Britain. It was a national institution as well as a nationalised corporation and it could not be ignored.

The glare of publicity might have intimidated a less determined organisation when in 1959 BEA decided it would have a new look. There were bound to be some cries of anguish, but the airline was a business concern as well as a national champion. The old image had served its purpose and after 13 years it was out of date. The emblem of the flying key was to disappear. Keyline House, headquarters of the corporation at Bourne School, was renamed Bealine House. The words 'British European Airways' were taken from the sides of all the aircraft, so was the flying key.

A plain red square containing the initials 'BEA' was neater, quicker and easier to read and more modern. The corporation's own crest, the centre of a storm when Mr Masefield had BEA's initials written across it, also disappeared from the sides of aircraft. So did the famous names and with them the prefix 'R.M.A.' signifying Royal Mail Aircraft. It was to be a clean sweep and the cost of tearing down old signs and erecting new ones, as well as repainting every aircraft, ran to thousands of pounds.

A rumble of complaints accompanied these reforms, but there were two other points which became focuses for criticism. The first was that the entire wing surfaces on all planes were to be painted a bright red. The new colour, on the tops and undersides of the wings, would make the aircraft more conspicuous—a safety factor—and would make the planes more readily identifiable as belonging to BEA. Passengers and air-minded MPs protested and one traveller said the colour made her feel ill. But the airline's official spokesman had been ready for criticism and answered it fairly and firmly. He was also prepared for the inevitable row about the last of the changes, the shrinking of the national flag.

The BEA logo in 1946

The 1959 'Red Square'

The BEA logo now in use

The Union Jack was to be removed from the tail fins and placed on the noses of the aircraft. In its new position the flag had to be reduced to half the original size so that it would be in proportion to the dimension of the fuselage. A roar rose from the House of Commons. Ten Conservative MPs quickly raised and signed a motion which said the House 'deplores the action of British European Airways in drastically reducing the size of the national flag on its aircraft, and in deleting altogether the words British European Airways, the corporation's crest, and the aircrafts' individual names'.

The other changes were of little importance. They had been thrown into the argument as makeweights. It was shrinking the national flag which sparked the controversy. Newspapers blazed the full glare of publicity on to the incident with cameramen swarming to Heathrow and other airports to photograph the offending designs.

But the critics had no footing. The safety angle could not be played up. The new look was seen to be a better proposition commercially and no-one could justify the charge that BEA was unpatriotic. In a carefully-worded answer, an official said:

'It is true that the full rigmarole title of the corporation is going out, but the letters B.E.A. are being put in three places on each side of the aircraft in more prominent position. The Union Jack is being placed on the nose of the aircraft where it can be seen at ground level, and the individual name of each plane will be put inside. No passengers ever notice the name on the outside. We think we are the most patriotic airline. We have staffed our British aircraft with British personnel, and in doing so have become the foremost airline in Europe. We think this is practical patriotism.'

It was its passengers that the airline cared about most and they were encouraged by a reduction in fares on domestic routes for a five-month winter period. At the same time a scheme under which staff could win bonuses for being extra helpful to passengers was announced. Prizes of up to £10 were awarded every three months for 'the most outstanding acts of service'.

Nine years later, the process of changing emblems was embarked upon again. This time the Union Jack was removed from the nose and a larger Union Jack type symbol put back on the tail. The dissenters were few; it seemed as if people had accepted at last that BEA knew what it was doing and where it was going. It might have been argued that spending £100,000 on changing a symbol was a waste of public money. But BEA had proved in the past that its commercial judgement on flags and emblems was sound and no-one was prepared to doubt the wisdom of the expenditure.

Much of the flying for BEA's pilots is routine. Unknown factors, such as changing weather conditions, have been removed by the speed of today's jets and the accuracy of forecasting, brought about in part by better communications. Pilots know what the weather is like at the ends of their journeys even before they take-off and because conditions can change while the plane is on its way, the flying crews are kept fully informed. Flying over the weather removes the unwanted challenge of a storm and the perils of icing up.

But the unexpected can creep up on a pilot and all the training he has received for emergency situations then becomes worthwhile. Had there been any danger to passengers in the Gibraltar crisis in 1967, BEA would have stopped flying planes to the Rock immediately. But the restrictions placed by Spain on the air space surrounding the colony made landings and take-offs even more exacting. While the political storm raged, Britain's sovereignty over the territory was being reaffirmed by its national airline. A BEA Comet flew to Gibraltar and it took a steady hand to keep the plane 200 yards away from the edge of the prohibited flying zone in Algeciras Bay while making the approach to the landing strip.

R.A.F. Hunter jets stood by to protect the Comet, which landed safely. On the return journey, the captain reported that he had been 'escorted' away from the area by two Spanish jets which had closed in at 400 mph and monitored the Comet's progress. The sabre-rattling continued for a year but BEA kept the Union Jack flying over Gibraltar. At one stage, the airline got fined by the Spanish Air Ministry because a Comet was said to have violated the prohibited flying zone. BEA denied the charge and a spokesman commented, 'The size of the fine is an indication of the importance of this incident.' The maximum penalty was £600. BEA was fined £12. Within a few months the whole episode was forgotten and chairman Sir Anthony Milward flew to Madrid to negotiate more flights to Spain and an increase in tourist traffic.

BEA had blazed many trails on behalf of Britain. It is usually the first to go in after an upheaval has shaken a European or Mediterranean territory, re-establishing links for all levels of society. The air link is the first necessity whether it is for flying in emergency supplies after a natural disaster or major accident, for evacuating refugees and bringing patriots home in times of war, or for maintaining contact with the outside world following a political crisis. The war in the Middle East stopped services to Tel Aviv and Beirut and planes were turned round at Athens. The war lasted seven days, but full schedules to both capitals were being run again by BEA after an interruption of only four days.

BEA stated publicly in 1951 that its aims were to satisfy its passengers, to look after its staff and to maintain economic, efficient and regular services. Ten years later, these aims were still being pursued, but with the rider:

'In the broader sense, our objectives are to play our part in the creation of a rising standard of living for the people in this country and of Europe, in the development of trade and commerce in and between the countries we serve, and in ensuring that this country leads the world in the field of air transport.'

Another ten years has seen BEA grow into more than an airline, more than a profit-making concern bringing in millions of pounds in foreign earnings, more than a show-case for British products, more than an ardent flag-waver and provider of a service. Along with BOAC it has discovered that being owned by the nation is one thing and that commanding the respect of its people is another.

THE TRAIL BLAZERS
A gallery of BEA planes through twenty-five years

Above: Several Junkers 52, renamed 'Jupiters', came to BEA from Germany as war reparations in 1946

Below: the Avro 19 was in service with BEA for 12 months after 1946

BRITISH EUROPEAN AIRWAYS

G-AHIG

Two versions of the Douglas DC-3 Dakota. Above: Pionair 'Charles Samson'. Below: The Dart Dakota

Above: The Viking 'Sir Bertram Ramsay' in flight. Below: The Elizabethan 'William Shakespeare'

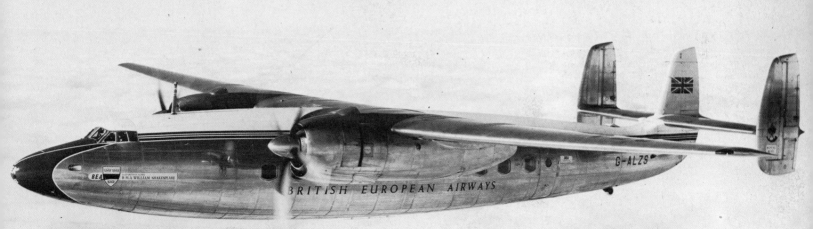

Viscount V 701, Discovery Class, 'Sir Robert Falcon Scott' (1953)

Right: Viscount V 802 showing the Red Square markings (1960)

84

Right: one of BEA's three Handley Page Heralds at the SBAC Show, Farnborough, 1959

Below: BEA's sole Bristol Freighter 21, photographed in 1951

Above: Argosy 222 taking off from Stansted (1965)

Below: De Havilland Heron 1B about to touch down

Above: Vickers Vanguard at Farnborough (1959)   Below: Vickers Vanguard 'Merchantman' in flight

A Hawker Siddeley Trident 1C (1967)

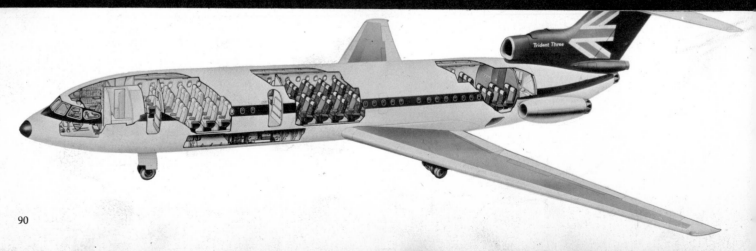

Above: Trident Three taking off. Below: cutaway diagram showing Trident Three interior

The BAC Super One-Eleven taking off from Hurn Airport on its maiden flight (February, 1968)

91

CHAPTER 6

No. 1 IN EUROPE

How MUCH is BEA claiming today by styling itself 'No. 1 in Europe'? Does it deserve the title, or does it go unchallenged by being the only state-owned airline engaged exclusively on European services? How big is BEA in the eyes of the rest of the world? Would it be running the largest number of air services in our continent without the protection on almost all international routes of pool partnership with European carriers?

Imperial Airways was the big name in British aviation before the war. It was formed in 1924 as the 'chosen instrument' of the British Government by the merger of four independent airlines—Handley Page Transport Ltd., The Instone Air Line Ltd., The Daimler Airway and British Marine Air Navigation Co. Ltd. Imperial got a Government subsidy of £1 million and built up a strong chain of regular routes which was handed over in 1940 when it was superseded by BOAC. In 16 years it flew more than 160 aircraft at one time or another and carried a total of 610,000 passengers. BEA carried 800,000 passengers in the month of July 1965 and recorded a massive 972,428 on scheduled services alone in August 1970. The figure that Imperial Airways achieved in its entire history can now be surpassed by BEA in just three weeks!

By 1959 BEA was second, behind Pan-American Air-

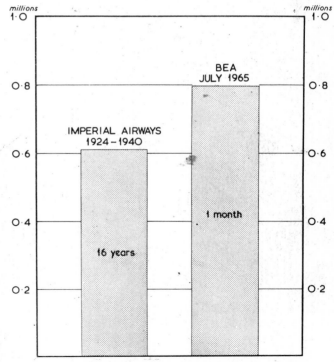

Chart showing the dramatic rise in passenger numbers since 1924

Left: Duty Officer Michael Fisher directs the queue of visitors to the Super One-Eleven at Tempelhof Airport, Berlin (1968)

ways, in the world league table of international passengers carried. Air France, which flies all over the world, was third with other European airlines in the next three positions. Ten years later BEA was still the second largest international carrier and seventh in a complete list of the world's airlines which included the giant American domestic carriers. On its 21st birthday, BEA was the only airline in Europe, with the exception of tiny Finnair, making a profit. More people travelled with BEA than with any other European airline. The sole exception was Aeroflot, Russia's national airline, which had and still has a monopoly inside the Soviet Union.

A massive total of 8,475,856 passengers were carried by the corporation in 1970, well over 5 million of them on international routes. More than 130,000 tons of freight was uplifted and 16,000 tons of letters and parcels. The fleet of about 100 aircraft make over a third of a million take-offs and landings a year at 85 destinations in the British Isles, the mainland of Europe, islands in the Mediterranean, in the Near and Middle East.

While other airlines in Europe and America were struggling for profits in 1970, BEA made a record £6,532,000. BOAC covers the long-haul routes around the globe and was even better off. But it has only half the number of planes and makes journeys of far greater length. BEA's problem has always been that the flights its aircraft make are among the shortest in the world. It is the take-offs and landings which cost money and the cruise portion in the middle where money is made. Roughly speaking, the longer the cruise, the easier it is to make the route pay. BEA is chained to the chores of Europe, but it has been exercised vigorously enough to make a handsome profit 13 times out of 16 since 1954.

By all normal business criteria, BEA must be adjudged as one of Britain's most successful concerns. Its total revenue in 1969/70 was £126,038,000. Despite massive losses in its first eight years, it is able to say that overall the first 25 years have been profitable.

There are many ways in which an airline can claim to be first. BOAC might be regarded in recent years as the most profitable airline in the world; United Airlines of America in the West and Aeroflot in the East as having the largest fleets; Pan-American Airways as carrying the greatest number of international passengers. Others can claim to fly farther in a year than anyone else, or to run more flights, or fly the most hours, or to have the largest unduplicated mileage on their networks. Independent airlines running charter flights and no scheduled services at all might claim that they fill more of their seats than anyone else.

But many of the comparisons between airlines are worthless. Each has a different job to do. So much depends on politics, geography and economic background. Yet if any assessment is made of Europe's airlines, of what they do inside their own countries and across the continent, of the money they make despite the unprofitable services they provide, of their efficiency, their regularity of schedules and punctuality of flights, it is probably fair to say that BEA has a right to be called 'No. 1 in Europe'.

One-fifth of Europe's air travellers fly BEA. Many of the other national carriers have long-haul routes to worry about as well as the short hops, but in Europe BEA is still the largest. It earns more than 15 million dollars a year in the United States and Canada, although its nearest port of call to North America is Shannon, Ireland. When American tourists come to Britain or the Continent, BEA makes sure it has got in first to capture their trade on flights between European countries.

When it comes to plain figures, BEA has a great record. But statistics alone are cold comfort; there are many other ways of leading the field. At least one fully qualified woman pilot has tried to join BEA, only to find the corporation considers flying commercial airliners to be a man's prerogative. The lady in question was aged 25, had six years' experience of flying fare-paying passengers with other airlines and had spent £3,000 on getting the best qualifications possible.

BEA's attitude was: 'We do not employ girl pilots because we don't think they do the job as well as men and many people would not be prepared to get on a plane if they knew a woman was at the controls. We know of no big international airline which employs women pilots on any scale.'

There are several points arising from these remarks. First, it is a matter of opinion whether or not women make as good pilots or car drivers as men. Physical strength is not a consideration in flying airliners today. Secondly, it is indeed true that large numbers of women pilots are not employed by any airline, but Aeroflot, some South American companies and two independent British airlines do have a number of women pilots. Thirdly. to dismiss women fliers on the grounds that money for training is wasted on a woman who gets married and has children, is to deny the dedicated ones the chance of following a chosen career. Amy Johnson might have had something to say about that.

Of course, BEA cannot please everyone. For a nationalised industry to win favour with the public and at the same time remain within the bounds imposed by Parliament is almost impossible. A traditional British compromise is often the answer, even if it does mean that the No. 1 position has to be forfeited.

There were good reasons why BEA did not lead the way with jet travel. Now it has found other reasons for sticking to turbo-props on domestic services. Air France got rid of the last of its propeller-driven aircraft in March 1971 and after 62 years went over to an all-jet operation. In the very same week BEA was trying to justify the retention of turbo-prop Viscounts on its Channel Islands routes.

Jersey senator Clarence Dupre, president of Jersey Tourism Committee and a member of the Channel Islands Air Advisory Council, said his island competed with places such as Majorca and that people wanted to travel the modern way. BEA had been very slow, he said, to bring in modern aircraft. Scheduled jet flights were banned in Guernsey but Jersey wanted jets.

The director of BEA's newly-formed Channel Islands division, Mr Ian Scott-Hill, lamented: 'Progress is a slow, uphill journey requiring enthusiasm, adaptability and perseverance. It would be nice to think that a "new technology" tailored aircraft lurked just around the corner which would dramatically improve the economics of short-haul. Unhappily this is not the case and best results are still obtained with old-fashioned turbo-prop types.'

Fewer than a million people a year travelled with BEA until 1952. But after 25 years the grand total is approximately 100 million. More than $1\frac{1}{2}$ million a year are now carried by BEA's German division. BEA operates 97-seat Super One-Elevens between Berlin and Frankfurt, Munich, Bremen, Stuttgart, Cologne/Bonn, Düsseldorf, Hanover and Hamburg. The services bring in more than £8 million annually, about nine per cent of BEA's total revenue. BEA aircraft take-off or land over 90 times a day at Berlin's Tempelhof airport, the airline's busiest station after Heathrow.

This airline within an airline results from a ban imposed at the end of the war on Germany having an airline or an air force. Lufthansa, the West German airline has subsequently been allowed to develop. But the Soviets insist that only the four occupying powers—Britain, France, Russia and the U.S.—can operate along the Berlin air corridors. Pan-American, Air France and BEA still have the rights, but the dispute over the sovereignty of the air space above East Germany and about the status of Berlin goes on. In April 1969 BEA began operating *combined* services with Air France from Frankfurt and Munich to Berlin and back to eliminate the fierce competition they were making for each other and to cut costs by pooling the use of ground equipment.

On some flights BEA *and* Air France stewardesses work side by side in BEA's Super One-Elevens, an arrangement which makes a crazy cocktail of co-operation and rivalry. One day it is almost certain that the internal German services will be handed back to Lufthansa. The West

Germans are already getting together with the Russians over flights from Frankfurt skirting East Germany to Moscow.

If Lufthansa does win back permission to fly to Berlin BEA might simply transfer its Super One-Elevens to the latest of its subsidiary companies, BEA Airtours Ltd. Airtours began its operations in March 1970 when the first Comet flight left Gatwick airport for Palma. The company was formed to allow BEA a slice of the lucrative inclusive tour market and its nine Comets carried some 600,000 passengers in the first year. In February 1969, six months before the formation of the company was announced, BEA was ready to sell its fleet of Comets to the highest bidder. It wanted around £500,000 each for the planes which would have been snapped up by charter airlines had BEA Airtours not been started.

The decision to start Airtours was immediately justified.

More than 350,000 seats on over 4,300 round trips to European holiday resorts were sold in 1970. Most of the flights leave from Gatwick, but Manchester and Birmingham airports are also used. The development of the new company is likely to to prove as important to BEA as almost any single decision its board has ever taken. Thousands more families are taking packaged tour holidays in Europe every year and BEA has 25 years of operational know-how to call on when flying them there. More than half the flights go to Spain, although 53 destinations including Sardinia, Turkey and Tunisia are served. The new company was started with a staff of 375, nearly all of them coming from the parent company. All but 28 were pilots, stewards and stewardesses, or engineers.

On its way to earning pride of place in Europe, BEA has won the Queen's Award for Industry and the Golden Tulip, the major award of the International Advertising

Association, for a campaign in Europe promoting air travel to Britain. A major international airline must do more than fly aeroplanes. It has to promote traffic by providing facilities such as BEA's marketing guide to Europe in which British businessmen can find a ready reference of basic information when selling on the Continent.

But first it must ensure that the obvious features about flying are right. The most important is booking seats. Sir Anthony Milward warned in 1966 that not every passenger made his reservation, bought a ticket and turned up at the airport for the flight on which he is booked. Many more: (a) made bookings but later cancelled them, the flight having become 'fully' booked in the meantime; (b) made bookings but failed to turn up for the flight; (c) bought tickets indicating bookings, but turned up to find the airline had not been told of the purchases; (d) turned up for flights on which tickets showed bookings, but were not booked because of an error in the chain of reservations.

Sometimes as many as one in five would make bookings and later cancel them, often with the minimum of notice before the flight. One in ten simply failed to turn up for flights on which they were booked.

There were four obvious solutions to the problem. Passengers could be charged for late cancellations or for not turning up. Flights could be operated with no seats reserved, simply taking those who turned up for a journey at an advertised time. Booking techniques could be improved so that errors and abuses of the system were reduced. The last choice was to have an automatic seat reservations system. The first three solutions had good and bad points. But an automatic system, while not solving all the problems, could make life easier for booking clerks and passengers. Used to its full advantage it would save time and money for its operator.

BEA's Beacon computer system came into action in 1965 and was only the fourth of its kind in the world, the others being in the United States. It is linked to 350 desks in the

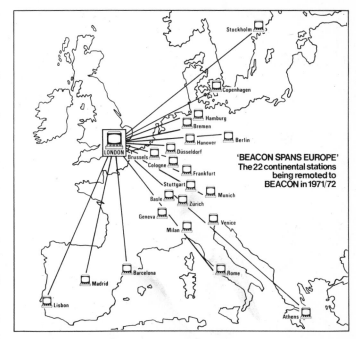

'BEACON SPANS EUROPE'
The 22 continental stations being remoted to BEACON in 1971/72

central booking office at West London Air Terminal and 250 more in major offices throughout Britain. Another 200 in 22 BEA offices spread around nine European countries will be hooked up by the end of 1972.

When a potential passenger arrives at or telephones a BEA booking office, the clerk can ask the computer if the wanted seat is available by operating the keys or push-buttons at his desk. He gets an answer within three seconds. If the answer is 'no', the computer lists alternatives and when a booking is made the computer subtracts the seats from the total on its file for that flight. If these are the last, it will tell the next enquirer, even if it is only seconds later, that the flight is fully booked.

Shortly before take-off the computer prints out a complete list of passengers including their personal details and special requirements. It can even tell the stewardess that a particular passenger wants a vegetarian meal. Unlike

Left: Businessmen disembark from a Super One-Eleven at Berlin, Tempelhof

Operating the Univac Reservations Equipment at West London Terminal

of soap, towels and meals. It has speeded up check-in procedures and cargo loading. The computer will soon be working as a master planner, bringing crews and aircraft together in the right place at the right time. Bad weather, illness affecting a pilot, or faults on aeroplanes can wreck plans for keeping aircraft busy. Beacon will be able to tell controllers the position within seconds. Overhauls and maintenance of aircraft are already being computer supervised. The safe life of aeroplane parts is monitored to make sure repair work is carried out in the correct order of priority. Beacon originally cost £5 million—by 1975 it will be saving BEA well over £1,000,000 a year.

The computer would be useless, however, without modern facilities for engineers, maintenance men and cargo handlers to go with it. A new cargo terminal at Manchester was opened in 1968 and improvements to those at Belfast and Birmingham followed soon afterwards. The £4 million cargo handling system at Heathrow was completed in September 1969. Work started on a new servicing hangar at Heathrow the previous month and an engineering apprentices school near the airport for BOAC and BEA employees was opened in March 1970.

From the passengers' point of view, BEA's 25th year brought a bigger and better aircraft. It was the Trident Three, the first of which went into service in April 1971. On the ground and without others to compare it against, the Three might be dismissed as just another Trident. It has the same wingspan as the Trident Two and at 131 feet 2 inches is less than 17 feet longer. It carries up to 140 people instead of a maximum of 115, but the difference is hard to spot even after you have stepped on board and looked around after fastening your seat belt.

But once it has started its take-off run, the difference is immediately noticeable. Jet-age passengers are accustomed to being pressed back in their seats by acceleration and steep climbs. The same thing happens in the Trident Three, but it is quite easy to feel the extra power. Acceleration is stronger, the jet seems to leap up from the runway and

the man in the central reservations hall faced with miles of paper, a queue for documents and a never-ending stream of telephone calls and teleprinter messages, the computer does not lose or muddle entries. It can easily alter or cancel them and can record details for a year ahead. Ten angry minutes of hanging on to a telephone has become an efficient operation taking as little as 20 seconds.

Beacon copes with more than 20 million bookings a year for BEA and subsidiary airlines. But computers can be programmed by an airline for many other purposes besides bookings. Beacon helps BEA with payrolls, aircraft maintenance control, ordering aircraft spares and even supplies

A fish-eye view of the Reservations Hall at West London Air Terminal

the climb is even more positive. It zooms towards the clouds and punches through them within seconds, popping up into the brilliant sunshine like a jack-in-the-box.

The reason for this faster getaway is a booster jet, an extra 'half-engine' which is opened up for take-off and climbing. The three main Rolls-Royce Spey engines are used for cruising, but the RB162 booster makes all the difference at the start of the journey. It means that the Trident Three can take-off from shorter runways. It can race clear of adverse weather more quickly and shrink out of earshot of people on the ground in less time. More power means greater flexibility and increased safety. BEA ordered 26 Trident Threes which are now the star performers among its galaxy of British-built aircraft.

The Trident fleet is the backbone of BEA Mainline, one of the new divisions created on 1st April 1971 by chairman and chief executive Mr Henry Marking. Mainline is responsible for scheduled services in Europe and trunk routes within Britain which radiate out of London. The Super One-Eleven Division operates the aircraft which gives it its title. It runs scheduled international and domestic routes from its Manchester base as well as being overlord for the German routes.

Scotland and the Channel Islands were given separate divisions, both of which run Viscounts. A Travel Sales Division and a Cargo Division were also formed. Each is a separate business.

The re-organisation was forced on BEA because of the size and scope of its interests. One of its most important subsidiaries is British Air Services which looks after Northeast and Cambrian Airways. BEA and BAS operate 80 per cent of the flights within Britain. Cambrian runs scheduled services in England, Wales, to the Republic of Ireland and to Paris—radiating mainly from Cardiff, Bristol, Liverpool and London—and also has an Isle of Man network. Northeast looks after Newcastle, Leeds/Bradford and other cities in the area.

The remaining divisions are formed from BEA Airtours,

BEA Helicopters (*see Chapter* 10) and Sovereign Group Hotels Ltd. BEA has discovered it *must* take an interest in the hotel business. Railways discovered the same need 100 years ago. Passengers would not travel on trains if there was nowhere for them to stay at the end of their journeys. The same goes for air travellers.

There has been an acute shortage of hotel beds not only in new holiday resorts but also in capital cities. BOAC, TWA and Pan-American have all found it necessary to go into the hotel business, either by forming subsidiaries and employing experts to run them, or by buying up existing hotel chains. BEA's policy has been to take substantial minority interests in companies operating hotels. It has links with the Excelsior hotels serving Manchester, Birmingham and Renfrew airports; the Phoenicia and Imperial in Malta, and the Plaza Athenee, George V and

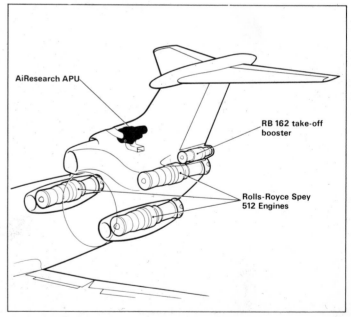

AiResearch APU

RB 162 take-off booster

Rolls-Royce Spey 512 Engines

The auxiliary power unit, engines and booster in the Trident Three tail

Fish-eye view of a Trident cockpit with Captain H J Booth (left) and Flying Officer J W Mahany

La Tremoille in Paris. With other airlines BEA created the European Hotel Corporation to develop a chain of modern hotels in major continental cities.

There are plenty of rooms fit for film stars and millionaires, but far from enough inexpensive accommodation. BEA's hotels have to pay their own way. But the Beacon computer is providing a link between BEA offices and 600 hotels so that rooms can be booked instantaneously. Sir Anthony Milward said in 1969:

'Nowadays we have to accept that we must be deeply involved in all the services that make up the complete business trip or holiday fortnight. We must be ready to provide an overall travel service including within it our previous role as simple point-to-point air carriers. A full and comprehensive overall travel service means, *inter alia*, seeing that passengers are provided with suitable accommodation at destination points, and this in turn can mean booking, buying or building hotel rooms as the case may be.'

BEA did not grow big by accident. Nor was it by chance that it took an interest in package tours, helicopters, subsidiary airlines, tourist promotions, cargo and in providing essential services and hotels. Nor is this the end of the story. Besides its stake in the College of Air Training, BEA has an offshoot which provides communications handling systems for all airlines and another for manufacturing, printing and publishing flight guides, maps and charts.

Once it was Alitalia and Aer Lingus which were associated airlines. Now BEA is fostering Cyprus Airways, Gibraltar Airways and Malta Airways in which it has 23, 49 and 34 per cent interests respectively. Cyprus Airways flies to London, Ankara, Beirut, Cairo, Istanbul, Rhodes, Tel Aviv and Frankfurt. Gibraltar Airways links the Rock with Tangier and runs charter flights to Morocco. The shuttle service across the Straits of Gibraltar was run by a DC-3 until 1970 when a Viscount replaced it. Malta Airways, for which BEA supplies flying crews and air-

craft, goes to Catania, Rome and Tripoli. All three airlines make small but useful profits.

While passengers are the No. 1 concern, BEA also cares for its 'family'. Hundreds of employees who began with the airline in 1946 are still there after 25 years. The total number has increased steadily year by year. The only cut back was in 1949 when redundancies were forced by re-organisation. BEA began with 1,641 people in August 1946 and then progressed to:

1947	5,731	1955	9,237	1963	16,036
1948	7,069	1956	10,198	1964	17,189
1949	6,324	1957	10,589	1965	18,011
1950	6,582	1958	11,301	1966	19,288
1951	7,279	1959	11,730	1967	20,619
1952	8,223	1960	12,502	1968	21,560
1953	8,558	1961	13,815	1969	22,232
1954	9,064	1962	15,383	1970	23,834

As in other airlines, employees who have been at their

BEA routes in 1946.
Compare these with present trunk routes (*opposite*)

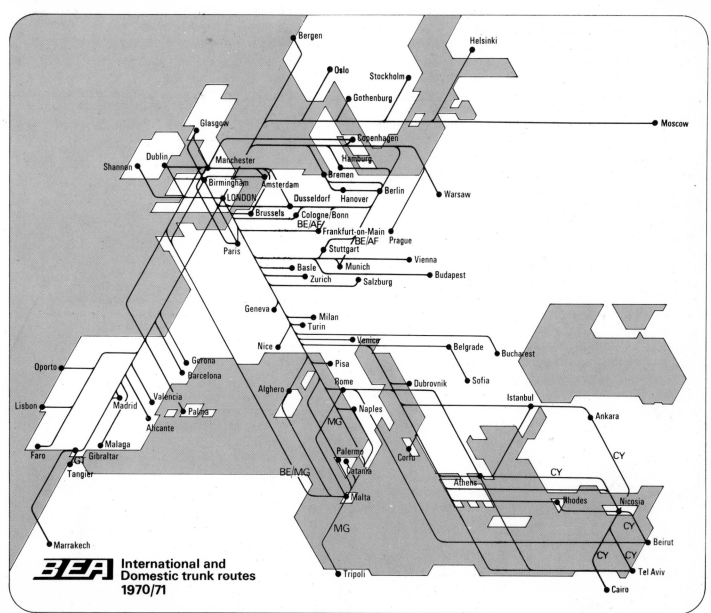

BEA International and Domestic trunk routes 1970/71

BEA's international and domestic trunk routes today

When you want to find out . . . at West London Air Terminal

jobs for a stipulated period can fly anywhere on the network for only a fraction of the usual fare. More important, the Airways Housing Trust Ltd. is a subsidiary of BEA and BOAC which bought land and held it for lease to the British Airways Staff Housing Society. Some 1,600 homes have been built by the Society in areas near Heathrow Airport.

Like any other major firm, BEA has had its share of staff problems. A captain of a Vanguard caused a stir in 1966 when he expressed 'shame and embarrassment' to passengers at having to apologise for a flight delay. The incident was investigated and closed, but a month later a group of pilots was grumbling over a series of problems ranging from engineering troubles to salaries. Once again the airline found itself flying through turbulence and in an effort to improve morale a weekly newspaper was started, a punctuality drive launched and top management shaken up to give junior executives more responsibility. In the meantime, eleven MPs were tabling a motion in the House of Commons warmly congratulating the corporation on the position it had achieved among European airlines, welcoming attempts to improve relations between staff and passengers and applauding orders for more British aircraft. It was the airline's 20th birthday.

The motion was a pat on the back for BEA, an encouragement for its staff and an unintentional reminder that airlines can never be far removed from politics. BEA's prominence in the aviation world can be seriously affected by Britain's policies and by foreign governments. BEA's managers abroad have to be ambassadors and diplomats as well as airline men. They must acknowledge national days in every European country as well as those at home. Staff in Morocco should know the day of the Festival of the Throne, those in Turkey must watch for the Seker Bayram celebrations and others in Hungary observe the traditions of October Revolution Day.

Sometimes an awkward situation arises which is none of BEA's making. Flights to Istanbul and Ankara were banned for a time at the end of 1969 because of a 'who lands where' squabble. Turkish Airlines, like any other carrier, wanted to use Heathrow airport when its services to London were about to begin. But the Government-owned British Airports Authority directed the airline to Gatwick. Heathrow was nearing saturation point and there was room at Gatwick, said the B.A.A. It was a matter of prestige to the Turks. Heathrow is the largest international airport in the world and those who use it guard their rights jealously. But to allow entry to one small airline and not another is politically dangerous. And should size matter? Why should an established airline from a large country be allowed in while new operators from developing countries are excluded?

This kind of situation is one over which BEA has no control. In the same way, it must tolerate political interference such as the instruction under which some of its routes, and others operated by BOAC, were given to Caledonian/BUA, the independent carrier.

Repeated attempts have been made to merge BEA with BOAC; but this is one move which BEA has resisted successfully for 25 years. At various times when one or other corporation has hit a bad patch, someone has suggested that the solution should be a joining of forces. Across the Channel, Air France does much of the work of Britain's two corporations. Lufthansa would do both jobs for West Germany if it was allowed into Berlin. Italy, Spain, Switzerland, Holland and other European countries also have but one flag carrier.

But both Britain's nationalised airlines are successful whereas others struggle. The work they do requires entirely different techniques and aircraft. Planes such as the Viscount, which can make money on almost any length of journey, happen once in a lifetime. Co-operation between BOAC and BEA is increasing, but it is likely to end there. The final word comes from Mr Marking. Two months after his appointment as chairman, he said: 'There will always be misguided people in this world who, from time to time, try to raise this old thing. It comes up every so many years, but one has learned to discount it.'

BEA uses Routemaster buses to shuttle passengers between West London and Heathrow

A comprehensive turn-out of aircraft in use on BEA's Scottish services in the early 1960's. On the tarmac at Renfrew Airport, as the Pionair (right) prepares for take off are the Viscount and the Vanguard (background) and the Herald and the Heron in the foreground

CHAPTER 7

FLYING WITHOUT A PASSPORT

THE KEEPERS of the lighthouse at Dubh Artach had been marooned on their lonely Atlantic outpost in the Hebrides for ten weeks. Gales lashed breakers against the isolated rock and dark clouds scudded overhead. Suddenly, the drone of an aircraft was discernible between shrieking gusts of the storm. A German Junkers threaded its way round the islands under a cloud base of 500 feet and swooped down to a mere 40 feet above the sea. Fifteen times the pilot banked round the lighthouse. The last circuit was so low that spray from the waves beating on the rocks cascaded over the windows. Two of the crew held a rear door open as the radio officer shot three packages out on to the rock platform. The keepers stood for a moment in disbelief. Then they dashed forward to grab the bundles before the waves snatched them into the sea.

The Junkers circled once more before turning for home. Its pilot could see the lighthousemen waving their thanks. It was their first delivery of food, newspapers and cigarettes for more than two months. The aircraft was one of BEA's latest acquisitions, one of a fleet from Germany handed over as war reparations. It had been fitted out with a dozen seats and was about to enter service with the name 'Jupiter'. The delivery made to the men at Dubh Artach in 1947 was no more than a bright idea by one of the crew

to make better use of a training flight. It was the beginning of 25 years of service by British European Airways to the inhabitants of the United Kingdom.

Many of the flights have been necessities which cost BEA money. But they will continue because they are vital to islanders and the isolated. It may seem strange that BEA and independent British airlines have fought more than once for the privilege of losing money on flights inside the United Kingdom. The main arteries are from London to Glasgow, Edinburgh, Belfast and out of Manchester and Birmingham. They have to compete with improving rail and sea links and sometimes the unyielding problem of all-British weather. The passengers are usually bunches of commuting businessmen rather than holidaymakers.

The airline which accepts these routes also finds itself flying the hops between islands and mainland, across the highlands and the Welsh hills, over natural and man-made barriers. They are all part of the service. They can be fun to the adventurous and necessary for local trades, but there is little profit in them. The distance covered by almost all internal flights is less than 500 miles and the average is just over one hundred. There are times when take-offs seem almost to merge into landings—the plane is either climbing or descending with no time in between for straight and level flight.

The remote landing strips are a far cry from the glamour of Paris, the bustle of Munich, Vienna's charm, Rome's warmth and the blue of the Mediterranean. But the little places have a romance of their own. Sometimes it is a question of strapping in your shopping basket so that the eggs will not break when the plane bumps across the grass. Thurso airport once consisted of a hangar, a garage-type petrol pump and a dog to clear the sheep from the runway.

At least ten private companies were engaged in running scheduled services in Britain when BEA began in August 1946. Seven months later the corporation, in accordance with the Civil Aviation Act, took over eight of them. It inherited two DC-3s, eight Jupiters, 13 Avro 19s, one DH84 Dragon, one DH60G Moth and no fewer than 39 Dragon Rapides. Two more firms were absorbed by April and another seven Rapides added to the fleet.

The first internal service by BEA was on 1st January 1947 when a DC-3 left Northolt for Glasgow via Prestwick. Shetland had been 26 hours from London by boat, train and various other means. Now it was only seven hours away. The islanders grumbled that bad weather too often prevented planes leaving Northolt! It meant that they could not get home from Edinburgh and Aberdeen, the stops made on the way to Sumburgh in the Shetland Isles.

BEA's route maps depicting services in the British Isles for 1947 and 1971 are little changed. Both show some 25 airports to which scheduled services are run. Links in Scotland are remarkably similar although it is now possible to cut out some of the intermediate stops. The same points in Ireland are served, but there are more direct routes from airports in England and the Channel Islands.

One of the first moves made by BEA was to cut its home network and confine it to 'those routes that were likely to prove economic or were provided to meet a special public requirement'. In October 1947 the following services were stopped:

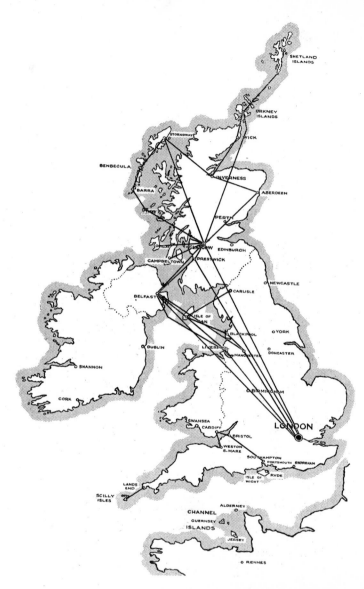

Domestic routes served by BEA at March 31, 1947

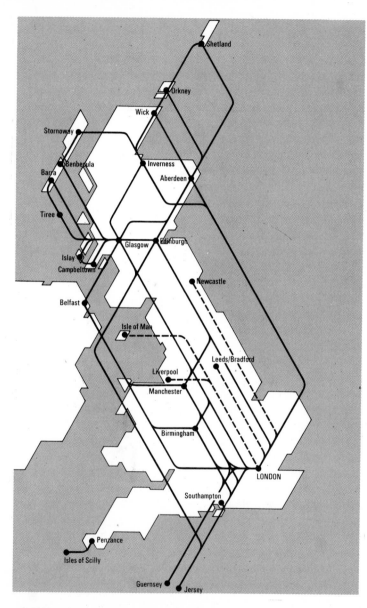

BEA's domestic routes today

Isle of Man/Carlisle
Cardiff/Bristol
Cardiff/Weston-super-Mare
Prestwick-Belfast

Belfast/Carlisle/Newcastle
Bristol/Southampton
Prestwick/London

Then services between Isle of Man/Blackpool, Glasgow/ Isle of Man and London/Guernsey were withdrawn for the winter months. There were protests and angry letters. More arguments followed when a review showed some fares were far too low and an average increase of 15 per cent was charged.

The pattern that had emerged on flights to Europe was now apparent at home. Airports were nearly deserted in winter but blossomed into life in the spring and summer. There was no better example than flights to the Isle of Man. BEA and others flew 58 services on weekdays and another 54 on Sundays to and from the island in summer. Rapides sprayed out on routes to Belfast, Blackpool, Carlisle, Glasgow, Liverpool and Manchester. A new direct daily service to London was soon to follow. Occasionally a DC-3 carrying four times as many passengers could be spared. There were long waiting lists for all flights and the overworked airport dealt with 338 flights on one June day in 1947. One of the biggest attractions with the introduction of the DC-3 was the novelty of refreshments served while you were actually in the air.

Only a trickle of passengers wanted to visit the Isle of Man in winter, however, and the cost of running an aeroplane could not be met by the fares of only one or two passengers. There were too few on winter flights between London and Edinburgh, so BEA cancelled this service as well. But the strength of the protests from the Scottish capital had them hastily restored. The first direct link between the capitals had been made in May 1947 when the airline's new chairman, Mr Gerard d'Erlanger, flew north in a DC-3. Newly-appointed staff and services controller, Mr Robert McKean (now director of the Scottish Airways division), discovered that the plane went on via

Aberdeen and Wick to Orkney, his ancestral homeland. A few days later he was able to make his first journey to Orkney. The islanders, he discovered, were much more air-minded than the mainlanders.

The size of some of the stations was minimal. Headquarters in the Scilly Isles was an old R.A.F. hut. A staff of three ran BEA's Cardiff base at Rhoose airport at one time. But Belfast was a larger base which expanded in summer. Ulster MPs found that with BEA's help they could go home for week-ends in Parliamentary time. The Northern Ireland airport quickly became the third busiest on the internal network with only Northolt and Heathrow handling more passengers.

The Channel Islands were also popular destinations. Flights increased when an inland grass runway at Jersey replaced the landing strip on the beach. Near the harbour where passengers came ashore after a nine-hour crossing by sea, a notice used to say, 'Fly BEA in exchange for your boat tickets.' A choppy sea was the airline's best friend. The cost of BEA's local air services spiralled in 1949. Mr G. O. 'Joe' Waters, general manager for British services, explained that costs could not be compared with those for continental routes. This was because (a) the stages flown were so short (average 113 miles); (b) landing fees were three times as high; (c) petrol tax was heavy; and (d) social services were grossly uneconomic when run to a regular timetable.

The biggest attraction in 1949 was the London–Jersey run which needed 61 Dakota flights a week. Glasgow was coming up fast, particularly as Vikings had been allocated to the route. Speed has always been the main attraction of air travel and of other forms of transport before it. In 1750 a stage coach took eleven days to reach London from Glasgow. Mail coaches cut the time to three days and railways reduced it to less than 24 hours in 1860. By 1935 the first air links brought the time down to 4½ hours and the Vikings were able to lower it to a little over two hours. Viscount, Vanguard and jets were to follow, each knocking

minutes off the previous best time. Today the flying time between the cities is 65 minutes.

BEA began to realise in the fifties that domestic routes were every bit as important as those to the Continent which got all the publicity. Some of the stations out of London had grown sufficiently to warrant direct flights to the Continent. Manchester was linked directly with Paris, Amsterdam, Dusseldorf and Zurich while Birmingham had a non-stop flight to Paris.

After seven years BEA was carrying three times as many passengers in Britain as it had done in its first year and losses on these routes had been reduced by 40 per cent. Once again, the Viscount was having an affect. So too, did cheaper winter fares. It came as a surprise to find six domestic routes in BEA's top ten and another four in the top twenty. The most popular routes in 1954/5 were:

ROUTE	PASSENGERS
London–Paris	235,430
London–Jersey	126,189
London–Glasgow	92,347
London–Belfast	77,887
Berlin–Hanover	72,798
Glasgow–Belfast	48,366
London–Dusseldorf	45,831
Berlin–Hamburg	45,126
London–Guernsey	42,611
London–Manchester	41,684
London–Nice	41,254
London–Zurich	40,907
Southampton–Jersey	40,066
London–Amsterdam	36,160
Liverpool–Isle of Man	35,704
London–Brussels	32,205
Manchester–Belfast	29,449
London–Edinburgh	29,167
Berlin–Dusseldorf	27,368
London–Geneva	26,236

Flights from London were the busiest because many passengers from outside the capital had no other means of reaching destinations abroad. Nevertheless there was a considerable amount of genuine local traffic. The Penzance–Scilly Isles service carried 22,230 passengers in 1954/5, more than London–Hamburg and other international routes. Manchester had its own links with the Continent and still showed a 49 per cent increase on the haul to London. Keen to maintain the inter-city traffic within Britain, BEA began a car hire scheme. Passengers could be met at the airport by an official who delivered the keys of a private car. Businessmen could drive round to a number of engagements in a day and return home the same evening.

But no matter how many new schemes were tried, the internal routes continued to lose money. More than a million passengers a year were being carried, almost as many as on international flights, but the local routes were losing £1,370,000 annually. It had been impossible to attract more people to fly in winter. The problem of seasonal traffic was highlighted in places like the Channel Isles where passenger figures for August (by far the best month) were eighteen times as high as for February (the worst month).

BEA has always operated the most reliable aircraft on domestic services—the tried and trusted planes which were 'handed down' from European services when they became too small or too slow. The aircraft have always had passenger appeal and it is often the case that more people per flight are carried on domestic services than on continental routes.

But low fares and the necessity for providing unprofitable links have always kept BEA's home runs in the red. The first problem it faced when the internal routes were acquired in 1947 was sorting out the motley collection of aircraft. Most were uneconomic, but suitable replacements were not available. The fleet of 45 Rapides dwindled to 19 in two years and a new type of small aircraft was sought.

The Rapides had been in operation since 1934 and a total of 685 were built. But they got the blame for 15 per cent of BEA's losses in the early years while carrying only 2 per cent of the passengers.

There were some places, however, where it seemed they could never be replaced. The last of the Rapides, nicknamed 'bamboo bombers', was still flying in 1964 for BEA. They earned a place in the hearts of Scilly Islanders where they were operating until the early sixties. While 500 mph jets zoomed thousands of feet overhead on transatlantic crossings, the Rapides were bobbing along below at 117 mph.

The 20-minute flight from Land's End would begin with a BEA employee beckoning through the window of the hut. The aircraft was parked a dozen paces away and passengers were distributed evenly about the cabin after a discreet sizing up of weight and build. Last to board was the pilot, muttering apologies as he squeezed his way through the tightly-packed cabin to the controls. If the wind was in the right direction, the take-off run would begin from where the plane was parked. The fabric on the wings glistened in the morning sun and the wind whistled through the struts.

Sometimes the local hunt would be followed for a mile or two, or a passing liner would be investigated before the pilot turned towards the islands. An average year would mean 5,500 flights for the three biplanes on the route, a total of some 20,000 passengers and an income of £44,000. In the winter, one plane would make three round trips a day and often face a 60 mph gale. In summer, an average day meant 20 round trips per plane. Local inhabitants joked that man would land on the moon before the Rapides were replaced. They were only a few years out.

The new transport for the Isles of Scilly was to be helicopters. Other domestic routes had intermediate stages. The DC-3 Pionairs gave way to Viscounts which brought a boom in passenger traffic. By June 1962, more passengers were being carried on the five principal air routes inside

A Heron air ambulance coming to the rescue at Barra

Britain than on any of the international runs apart from London–Paris. Top of the list was London–Glasgow with 362,000. Then came London–Paris 334,000; London–Belfast 267,000; London–Manchester 266,000; London–Jersey 210,000; and London–Edinburgh 201,000.

Scotland welcomed the Viscount just as every other country had done. It had seen the DC-3, the Viking and even an occasional Elizabethan on the main routes to London. Several smaller types appeared on the 'social services' to the highlands and islands. But they never went south of the border and at times it was as if Scotland had an airline of its own.

BEA has flown to Campbeltown, Islay, Tiree, the Outer Hebrides, Orkney and Shetlands ever since it first embarked on the duty of running domestic flights. It has used Rapides, Jupiters, Dakotas, Herons, Heralds and Viscounts on highlands and islands duties. The fleets which fly these routes mingle with the bigger aircraft at Glasgow Airport. A rare moment in the early sixties was captured when a Herald, Heron, DC-3, Viscount and a Vanguard appeared together at the terminal.

The best known of Scotland's services is that provided by the Air Ambulances. Hundreds of men and women owe their lives to the determination of a Scottish doctor and BEA. Ferrying sick patients from the islands by air was started by the doctor in Islay in 1933. In these remote

Safely at Barra, the Heron takes on the patient – and the mails

areas it was the only practical means of getting a man to hospital, particularly when the sea was rough. The crossing by boat from Islay to the mainland took ten hours and many patients did not survive it. BEA took over responsibility for the Air Ambulance service in 1947 and reorganised it in 1949. Rapides were used at first and in 1949/50 271 patients were flown in, many of them at night and in bad weather. The Rapides have now been replaced by four-engined Herons which cruise at 165 mph.

In the early hours of the morning on 28th September 1957, a Heron answered an Air Ambulance call to a seriously ill woman at Islay in the Inner Hebrides. The weather on the island was atrocious and in attempting to land, the Heron crashed. The crew of two and a nurse who was with them died instantly. In the same year over 50,000 miles were flown, carrying 304 sick people on 232 flights.

The nurses come from the Southern General Hospital, Glasgow, and take courses in aviation medicine, emergency procedures and survival. They are presented with certificates and silver 'wings' badges by BEA. The Air Ambulances have now flown over one million miles. They carry on average 300 patients a year. Costs of £12,000 annually are borne by the Scottish hospital boards.

The planes are based at Glasgow Airport.

More than 80 per cent of the calls come from Kintyre and the Western Isles, but patients are also collected from

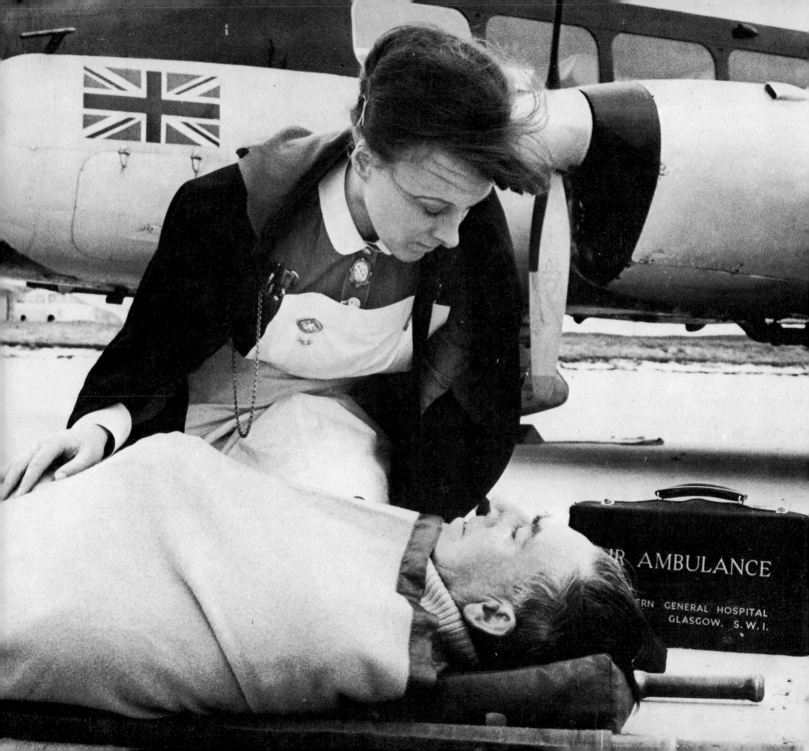

Orkney, Shetland, Wick and Inverness. Special stretcher equipment is fitted into the 14-seat Herons and at least one of the planes is available 24 hours a day. Occasionally, a Viscount is used. The decision to call out the Air Ambulance is made by the patient's doctor who has to consider not only the clinical urgency, but also the road the sick person must travel to get treatment.

BEA has a plane airborne within an hour. Two pilots and a nurse have to be called. The nurses volunteer for the service and a group of them stands by for flights which are made in off-duty hours. Special oxygen equipment and cots for babies are provided in the plane. Several babies have been born in the air on ambulance flights. A conventional road ambulance is waiting at the airport when the plane returns.

While one of the Herons waits for emergency calls, the other operates scheduled services from Glasgow to the islands of Tiree and Barra. Tiree has a concrete runway and landing the 5½-ton plane is a routine operation.

But the landing strip at Barra is the beach. Traigh Mohr, the Great Beach, more commonly known as the Cockle Strand, is a strip of rolling white sands smoothed by green Atlantic rollers. The only advice offered by inhabitants of Barra to new pilots is to make sure the knees of the seagulls standing on the beach are visible! There have been occasions when the sand has been too wet. An unwary pilot finds that by the time he has taxied to a standstill, his wheels have sunk in over the axles or even deeper.

There are few trees on the island, but plenty of malt whisky and pickled cockles. The most famous house is one overlooking the Cockle Strand where Sir Compton Mackenzie used to live. It was here that he wrote the book *Whisky Galore* and the film of it was shot locally. Lack of public transport has its problems, but there was a time when the two BEA officials made their three-mile journey to work at the beach on the airfield fire tender. Some passengers flying to Barra have found their plane deviating from its route so that they can look into the roaring mouth of Fingal's Cave on the Isle of Staffa.

In Scotland the Herons have outlasted the Handley Page Heralds which were able to take-off from very short runways. It was hoped that the new twin-engined plane might reduce losses on the Scottish mini-links. Despite the enormous publicity surrounding Prince Philip's tour of South America, the Herald did not catch on. BEA used its three Heralds for four years in Scotland, but runway improvements in 1966 allowed Viscounts to move in. The Heralds were then returned to the Ministry of Aviation which had loaned them to the corporation.

Viscounts were at work on most of BEA's internal services by this time and facing a new threat. Improvements to tracks and rolling stock had allowed British Rail to fight back with 100 mph trains. BEA had no wish to compete with another nationalised industry, so long as a service was provided, and cut back some of its flights. But the spur which forced them into renewing the services and to use jets in Britain was competition from the independent airlines which included British United Airways, Caledonian Airways and British Eagle.

BEA brought in the Vanguard on routes from London to Scotland and in order to make sure the customer was satisfied, the corporation quizzed him about flying. More than 60,000 questionnaires were handed out to passengers asking them the reasons for their journeys, convenience of flying times and for other information. Three years later a second attempt was made to achieve satisfaction by asking travellers in the same way. This time it was quite clear that whatever else was in demand, passengers preferred jets.

Sir Anthony Milward commented, 'The turbo-prop no longer seems so attractive as jets to passengers. It is due to what a friend of mine describes as the sex appeal of jets.' The jets can also chip off 15 minutes from the London–Glasgow time of a turbo-prop. It can make all the difference to passengers who want to catch connecting flights.

The pattern of BEA's domestic services has changed

little in 25 years. Money is still being lost, fares are still lower than for journeys to the Continent of the same distance. The Highlands and Islands network lost £339,000 in 1969/70 and the Channel Islands routes £1 million. But well over three million people travel BEA inside Britain. Many of them use internal flights as feeder services to London in order to fly abroad. The increase in passengers at home from 1966–69 was much smaller than that of previous years. It was not reflected in the numbers travelling on international flights.

Now that Scotland, the Channel Islands, Super One-Elevens at Manchester and Mainline flights have been made separate divisions, there is a renewed attack on the problem of making domestic services pay. The divisions will still have the benefit of being part of a large national-ised concern, but they are also able to compete against each other. This does not mean the corporation has forgotten Mr Masefield's motto of the early fifties: 'Our passengers are the purpose of our business not an inter-ruption of our work.' Nor does it prevent services such as the Air Ambulance being, as the anonymous writer put it in the 1966 annual report, 'dear to BEA's heart'. BEA chairman Mr Henry Marking said when announcing the new structure: 'I believe that people work better and more happily in smaller units, and I think staff will enjoy being associated with their particular unit and take pride in it. This should be particularly so in Scotland and the Channel Islands where for the first time since BEA took over the routes, their very proper traditional pride in having their own units can be recognised.' The complete tables show the steady growth BEA has achieved at home and abroad since it began. Passengers carried by BEA in twelve months ending 31st March were:

YEAR	DOMESTIC	INTERNATIONAL	TOTAL
1947	12,559	58,618	71,177
1948	361,311	150,211	511,522
1949	370,841	206,281	577,122
1950	398,089	353,423	751,512
1951	431,676	507,910	939,586
1952	486,203	649,376	1,135,579
1953	620,152	779,970	1,400,122
1954	754,052	902,727	1,656,779
1955	860,510	1,013,806	1,874,316
1956	1,029,488	1,195,259	2,224,747
1957	1,118,288	1,342,777	2,461,065
1958	1,234,108	1,531,483	2,765,591
1959	1,190,814	1,637,901	2,828,715
1960	1,425,484	1,864,122	3,289,606
1961	1,783,648	2,207,309	3,990,957
1962	2,111,586	2,281,792	4,393,378
1963	2,385,406	2,529,521	4,914,927
1964	2,583,590	3,021,222	5,604,812
1965	2,793,498	3,325,636	6,119,134
1966	3,023,544	3,819,219	6,842,763
1967	3,063,801	4,260,169	7,323,970
1968	3,067,985	4,266,977	7,334,962
1969	3,075,620	4,653,034	7,728,654
1970	3,148,751	5,327,105	8,475,856

Domestic services began in February 1947 so the figure of 12,559 is for two months only. International flights started in August 1946 and the figure of 58,618 is therefore for an eight-month period.

Right: the West London Air Terminal, opened in 1963

Above: boarding a Trident Three.   *Right: disembarking from a Trident Two*

Two crew members with their Airtours Comet — and a special welcome for a young Trident Three passenger

Left: strip-down maintenance check for a Trident

Above: pilot's eye view of the cockpit of a Comet 4B. The instrument panels give a good idea of the complexities of modern passenger aircraft

Right: from the chef at the London Airport Catering Centre to your 'table' on the aircraft. A progress report from the captain. And then it's time to relax

A BEA Heron taking off from the beach at Barra in the Outer Hebrides

CHAPTER 8

THE INSIDE STORY

YOU STEP INSIDE the Trident jet at Heathrow from a raised landing which has been extended to the side of the aircraft. The 'host' and 'hostess' greet you at the door. He is a steward with enough gold braid on his uniform to make you feel important. She is a stewardess with a warm smile that makes you feel at home. The cabin is cosy and discreetly lit. Background music plays softly. All the safety belts have been straightened tidily across the seats. There is not really enough room, but you are cheerful—travel is exciting and the reception they gave you is friendly.

The seats are in rows of six, three on either side of the aisle. You are not quite sure which is the 'best' and it hardly matters because they all look alike. Inexperienced travellers choose the ones nearest windows for sightseeing and photography. Old hands prefer ones next to the aisle so that they can get up without disturbing anyone, and order another drink more easily. No-one wants the seat in the middle of the three. It is always the last to be filled.

Daily or evening newspapers are brought round. You are asked if you would like a drink after take-off. The public address system clicks and the stewardess announces details about the flight in English and at least one other language. The broadcast ends with a request to fasten your seat belt ready for take-off. You know that it is a *safety* belt, but the timid must not be alarmed by such thoughts at this moment, so it is called a *seat* belt.

Everything seems new and fresh. It is as if the curtain is about to rise at the beginning of a show. So it is, but you should have seen the place half an hour ago. The plane had only just returned from the Continent. Vacuum cleaners were humming, old newspapers were scattered everywhere, ashtrays bulged. Metal wheeled trolleys stuffed with dozens of meal trays were being shoved into position as the chief steward checked them. All those seat/safety belts were flung aside and many of the seats had been thrown forward. Hand basins had to be cleaned, new towels and soap provided. Pilots were still collecting information on the weather, fuel and aircraft's weight. Stewardesses were picking up lists of the passengers' names and checking on special requirements.

Space is your main worry. You cannot put heavy brief-cases or bags on the coat rack in case they fall off and hit someone on the head. There is never enough room by your feet. Time is the main concern of the crew. The pilot finds his plane is in a queue waiting to take-off and there are headwinds so he will have to 'open the taps'. The steward is thinking about those drinks you ordered, the duty free buys you will want to make and of how soon to start

'Whisky and soda, sir'. On board a Dakota in 1949

A quick rubber aboard a Vickers Viking

serving the 100 lunches. This is the jet age. You are going by air because it is so much quicker. BEA has provided a jet and the crew have got to hurry or it will be time to land.

It was not always like this. Twenty-five years ago there was time to spare. Many a day for a steward or stewardess would begin by thumbing a lift from Park Royal, Hangar Lane, or other underground stations West of London. Buses to Northolt were few, particularly in the early morning, late evenings or on Sundays. No-one seemed to be able to get enough petrol to run a private car. The uniforms of BEA staff were soon recognised by drivers.

The A40 to Oxford passed the gates of the airport and hitch-hiking was no problem.

Once at Northolt, collecting passenger lists and checking the aircraft meant filling in forms and endlessly waiting. But there were only a dozen passengers at the most on an Avro 19 or Jupiter flight and there was time to talk to each one individually. Royal blue furnishings in the Jupiters replaced the austere interiors which paratroopers had had to sit staring at. BEA pilots found the German planes stable, light on the controls and placid. They could be landed at less than 60 mph, less than half the landing speed of today's jets.

Elbow room becomes more generous with the Elizabethan

Jupiters were solidly built and gave a feeling of confidence in bad weather. But passengers could be unnerved by the jangling of coil springs in the undercarriage when taxiing. The cabin heater, which could only be switched on after a speed of 80 knots had been achieved, gave a worse fright. It came into operation suddenly with a blood-curdling shriek and blasts of hot air rushed up through vents in the floor. Stewards found it worthwhile to brief passengers about the heater and the plane's other peculiarities before a flight began.

The interior of the Avro 19 also had single seats dotted along the fuselage. The main spar for the wings jutted up across the aisle and was easy enough to step over for those who realised it was there. The toilet was no more than an Elsan partitioned off by an innocent-looking, brightly coloured curtain. Vibration and noise in the Viking, the first new type of aircraft to be bought by BEA, were minimised so that passengers could hold conversations while flying. Rubber cushioning around the main spar where it passed through the fuselage made flying and taxiing smoother.

There were more than 20 passengers in the Viking with seats in rows of threes arranged in doubles and singles on either side of the aisle. Six of the seats faced the rear and so it was possible to have a foursome for bridge. It was with some pride that BEA told its passengers that in a Viking each of them would have a reading lamp, book rack, ashtray, cool air supply and electric service bell. Many journeys on the corporation's network lasted more than six hours. It was as well to get comfortable. The planes were not pressurised and had to fly through the bad weather rather than above it.

The question of rearward facing seats troubled BEA and other airlines for a time. Nearly all passengers preferred facing the front, although many experts said it was safer the other way around. But the Viking and the DC-3 sat back on their tails and some passengers found it uncomfortable to be 'falling out' of their seats when the plane taxied or climbed. The Royal Air Force uses VC10s, Hercules, Britannias and other large planes for ferrying troops and civilian personnel over the longest journeys. All the seats in R.A.F. planes today face the rear.

BEA followed up Vikings with Elizabethans and Viscounts which both had tricycle undercarriages allowing the fuselage to remain level with the ground. The first 18 of the Elizabethan's 47 seats were arranged in four rows all facing the tail. At least one survivor of the Elizabethan crash at Munich in 1958, a journalist, is convinced he owes

Mealtime on a modern Trident Two

his life to the fact that his seat faced backwards.

The arrival of jets changed the arguments, however. Fierce acceleration on take-offs and steep climbs deterred BEA and other airlines from placing seats the 'wrong' way round. Even when landing, jets fly nose high and rearward facing seats are uncomfortable. Jets are far more reliable than piston engines. High take-off and landing speeds probably negate the safety element in rearward facing seats.

Altering a seating layout is a simple matter. Sections of

the Trident can be converted from first-class seating (two abreast) to tourist class (three abreast) in a matter of minutes. Other planes had seats which could be folded against the side of the fuselage to make way for cargo. Today's armchair-type seat can be removed with ease. Seats are usually pitched 31–34 inches apart in tourist class and 42 inches in first-class cabins. Pitch is the distance between the front of one seat and the front of the seat behind it.

The allocation of seats is an awkward problem for BEA, an airline with many extremely short and heavily

FOR THE FIRST TIME EVER

HOT MEALS

DURING FLIGHT

ARE BEING SERVED ON ALL

BEA AEROPLANES

FROM MANCHESTER AND BIRMINGHAM

TO PARIS

BRITISH EUROPEAN AIRWAYS

Hot food for the first time (1952)

booked flights. Passengers have repeatedly asked to be able to reserve favoured seats on planes, probably because they do not want the middle seat of three and do not want to scramble to be first to one of the others. But allocating seats is a lengthy process particularly when the airport is busy and flights of more than 100 people are leaving every ten minutes. Nevertheless, BEA has introduced systems of reserving seats on most of its routes.

There were no undignified rushes for seats in the days of Northolt, but passengers faced other problems. Early flights to Germany had to rely on food supplies from the Navy, Army and Air Force Institute. Food rationing meant that items such as ham, cheese and eggs were almost unobtainable. The luckiest passengers got a lunch box in which they found sandwiches, rolls, fruit and fruit cake. Stewards had to make sure that their planes had sufficient hot water, coffee and milk. Then it was a question of balancing a tray on your knee and ignoring the air pockets which unexpectedly rocked the plane. Caterers had their moments at Northolt, too. One frosty January morning the lights failed in the kitchens. All work had to stop until the doors to the building were opened so that tractors and lorries could be driven up to shine in their headlights.

Stewards collected clean crockery, cutlery and trays before boarding their aircraft. Then there were rugs to be distributed, glasses to be put in their racks and hot water poured into a tank for the tea. There was much criticism in May 1947 when BEA decided to charge passengers for meals and light refreshments. It was thought that rival airlines would follow suit, but BEA were not then the leaders in Europe and the competitors showed no inclination to follow them. By March 1948, public opinion had made BEA think again on continental routes and two months later meals on internal routes were also free of charge.

The first hot meals served by BEA came in 1952 when improved catering was needed to go with the new kinds of aircraft about to be introduced. There were many diets to consider and members of some Eastern sects occasionally discovered there was nothing on board that their religions would allow them to eat. By 1957 BEA was serving up 4½ million meals in aircraft, restaurants, buffets and cafeterias throughout Europe. In another three years they were dealing with two million main meals, three million light meals and five million non-alcoholic drinks a year. The airline could not cope, and outsider caterers were brought in to take over the restaurants, cafés and bars. A new flight catering centre was opened in 1963 at Heathrow for aircraft meals. It had vast larders of bonded stores, food and soft drinks.

Washing-up was soon costing £100,000 a year and experiments were made with throwaway plastic cutlery. Cabin staff were instructed to watch carefully and note passenger's reactions. Anything which could save space or time could save money, but the bright ideas were not always popular. The Milk Marketing Board told its staff not to fly BEA after the airline had begun using skim milk powder. Then came protests that champagne at 6s (30p) a quarter bottle was extremely palatable, but not when it was served in plastic tumblers.

Today's demands from passengers include special meals for special days. Burns Night suppers on flights to Scotland would be incomplete without haggis. The traditions of saints days and other celebrations have also to be observed. And it is as well to mix diplomacy with drinks—Cyprus sherry out of Nicosia, hock available on planes to Germany, champagne and plenty of vin ordinaire out of Paris. Not everyone was pleased in 1959 when BEA stopped giving out boiled sweets, barley sugar or mints before take-off to prevent ears popping. An official said: 'The issue of sweets followed a recommendation by a body of doctors in 1946 when few of our aircraft were pressurised. That was 13 years ago. Now with full pressurisation, comparatively few people suffer from ear trouble.'

The subject was raised in the House of Commons in 1965 when a sweet-toothed MP complained that other airlines were still issuing his favourite barley sugars. He, too, was told the practice was no longer necessary. No-one raised the point that some passengers get nervous during take-offs and sweets help to lubricate dry mouths.

BEA did not lag behind in its catering, however. It was the first airline to have reclining seats with tables on the backs and the first to open a fully integrated flight catering centre. BEA led the way in chlorinating aircraft water supply systems to make water taken on board from any country safe to drink. It introduced the process of sand-blasting wine-bottle labels to solve the old problem of scratched or missing identifications and it even hired experts to advise on dishes such as smorgasbord.

There was little to choose between airlines once flying times and fares had become identical and planes were similar. Cabin service was the only way of being different. One BEA Comet captain refused to pass his jet ready for take-off when he found dirty footprints on the carpets. But when it comes to providing a service in the air, today's cabin crews have no time to spare. They have five times the number of passengers their forerunners had and there is only half the amount of time in which to serve everyone. Some full meals have shrunk to snacks and on some short flights snacks have given way to a quick drink.

Restrictions on duty-free liquor and tobacco imposed by Customs and Excise were scrapped in 1964 and BEA was then able to offer the same bargains as other airlines. Bans imposed by the airline itself on smoking pipes and cigars in passenger cabins were lifted in January 1965.

Attention to detail paid dividends. First-class passengers might notice that there is a right way and a wrong way to serve toothpicks. BEA memorandum No. 568 issued in 1967 was explicit. It read: 'At the end of each meal service, the steward will empty the contents of one pack (ten toothpicks) into a 3oz. glass. He will place the glass on a round sideplate and offer the toothpicks to his passengers. The toothpicks will be packed in Cellophane bags, each of which will contain ten toothpicks. One pack will be issued

for each sector to be operated. It is essential, therefore, that the steward uplifts the correct number of packs to ensure that he is able to offer toothpicks on each sector he will operate until he returns to base.'

Announcements over the public address systems in BEA aircraft were improved in the same year when stewardesses were taught microphone techniques and began reading out flight information. This duty had previously been performed by stewards or flight crew. One MP complained that announcements on domestic flights were unnecessary and interrupted him while he was working.

BEA now uses pre-recorded announcements in different languages on many continental services. More than a dozen were in use by 1970. Nearly all the stewards and stewardesses can speak a foreign language and some are fluent in three or four. The ability to speak a particular language is signified by a language flashes on the sleeves of uniforms. These badges are usually the flags of the countries concerned. Cabin staff are paid a 50p bonus a week for each language they can speak. A total of 21 badges are issued; they include most European languages as well as Arabic, Turkish, Hebrew and Urdu. There is also a badge for the deaf and dumb sign language.

The job of airline stewardess once was thought to be one of the most glamorous in the world. All the passengers were rich, famous or both and there were very few of them. The girls came from wealthy families or had relatives working for airlines. They would accompany their select band of travellers across the world in a plane which seemed to stop everywhere. There was time to talk, and to entertain in the evenings during overnight stops.

No wonder the ambition of almost every young girl after the war was to fly with an airline. BEA was receiving 25 letters a day in 1950, but interviewing a mere 450 of every 9,000 applicants. There were fewer than 30 vacancies a year and a poll among passengers showed 55 per cent were in favour of male attendants. The few girls that did get jobs found conditions changing, particularly if they worked for BEA. Manchester and back, perhaps twice in a day, was not what they had envisaged.

Nor was it easy to work in the limelight. The passport of a stewardess is her appearance and not everyone agreed about BEA's girls in the fifties. Two were suspended for smoking in public in 1953. It was a staff order that uniformed personnel should not sit about in the public sectors of airport buildings nor be seen smoking, and the two girls had done both. Another group was reprimanded for carrying overnight bags which advertised other airlines. The girls said they could not afford 15s (75p) charged by BEA for night-stop bags.

On another occasion several girls were warned against using eye shadow. It had been a 'long-standing rule' that ground staff and cabin crew should not wear excessive make-up. Even nail varnish was frowned upon. One of the girls remarked with a giggle, 'I was told eye shadow could not be overlooked!' Male receptionists, never mentioned by the press or on radio and television, complained that the public did not know they existed. It was always the girls who got the publicity.

The pay for a stewardess was a few hundred pounds a year, but it did not seem to matter. The job gave girls the chance to travel, to meet famous people and to be the envy of friends. It was the next best thing to being a film star or a model. But by 1960 there was no longer any doubt about the work. It was hard and often boring. A BEA official said, 'Any glamour attached to the work is mainly in the imagination of the public.' Today, most of the girls know what they are going in for. Stewardesses stay on average two years and two months with BEA. Stewards average $5\frac{1}{2}$ years.

The first uniforms worn by BEA stewardesses were ex-service supplies—the navy blue overlapping style worn by the Women's Royal Naval Service. New civilian uniforms followed. BEA tunics were simple, three-button designs with patch pockets and no belt. The tricorn hat looked attractive, but it funnelled rain down the backs of

Food being prepared at the Flight Catering Centre, Heathrow

Above: sleeve braid of BEA Captain, Senior First Officer, First Officer and Second Officer; captain's cap (left) and cap for other officers with BEA Wings

Below: Jacket sleeve, hat and brevet of BEA Stewardess. Sleeve markings indicate these ranks: 4 stripes: Duty Officer (non-flying); 3 stripes: Administrative Officer (non-flying); 2½ stripes: Chief Stewardess; 2 stripes: Stewardess Grade One; 1½ stripes: Stewardess Grade Two

134

Arabic
Czechoslovakian
Danish
Dutch
Finnish
French

German
Greek
Hungarian
Italian
Norwegian
Polish

Portuguese
Russian
Spanish
Swedish
Turkish
Serbo-Croa

Evolution of the BEA stewardess's uniform: 1947, 1954, 1960 and 1967

the girls' necks and in 1950 it was replaced by a forage cap type.

Blue uniforms remained the fashion for little more than a year before the board of directors decided to put the girls into grey barathea in winter and a lightweight fawn gaberdine in summer. Men's uniforms were changed to grey, too. Suits for pilots, cabin staffs and ground hostesses were still being individually tailored after the first four years, but in 1950 ready-to-wear uniforms became available.

Less than a year after going grey, the uniforms for male

The Queen meets the crew of a Viscount (1957)

Princess Margaret returns from Oslo on a Viscount (1961)

ground staff were changed back to blue. Nine thousand square yards of grey cloth was offered to BEA's 6,500 employees at 35s (£1·75) a yard. Even senior captains on £1,100 a year said they could not afford it. Questions in Parliament were bound to follow. What was the reason for the quick-change act, Minister of Civil Aviation Lord Pakenham was asked. It was a matter for the corporation, he said, although it was quite clear to the House of Lords that the change of colour had followed a change of leadership.

The stewardesses got a new jacket style of uniform by 1954 and five· years later, skirts were shortened. Lady Douglas, wife of BEA's chairman and a former model,

suggested to her husband that the women traffic clerks and stewardesses looked unfashionable. Their skirts, she said, should be shortened to two or three inches below the knee. The new look became official within 24 hours.

Other changes followed immediately. Hip-length jackets buttoning up to the neck came in with straight skirts and a modified forage cap style of hat without a cockade. The design was the result of a competition among students from the Royal College of Art. The airline had begun flights to Moscow and girls on the route were issued with ear muffs, ski-pants and lambs wool-lined boots.

New uniforms for stewardesses and passenger service girls designed by Hardy Amies were provided in 1968.

Left: The joke we'll never know. The Duke of Edinburgh inspects the Beacon reservations system

Prince Charles leaves Heathrow for Malta (1969)

The overcoats were a distinctive red. A standard all-wool pinafore dress in a choice of four colours came two years later for counter staff. Pilots' uniforms were traditional three-button jackets and these were replaced by double-breasted two button jackets. Single-breasted raincoats for pilots and stewards replaced the old military type which had lasted for 24 years.

Regulations governing improper dress are still observed. An advertisement in 1969 showed a sexy-looking girl welcoming people aboard a plane under the headline, 'Our Birds Fly to 89 Places in Europe.' One of the stewardesses wrote to complain. She objected to being called a bird and to the way the model wore her coat zipped half-way, her blouse collar sticking out and her hat at an angle. 'If I reported for a flight like that I would be reprimanded—and rightly so,' said the stewardess.

While skirt lengths, colours and styles change constantly the air girls are pleased that BEA has retained the

Some of the famous who travelled BEA in its earliest days. Above: Somerset Maugham. Top right: Laurence Olivier and Vivien Leigh. Right: Joan Collins

In from Montreux: Noël Coward. Off to Naples: Gracie Fields. Off to Madrid: Alec Guinness

brevets. They are proud of the wings which show they are on flying duties. Those promoted to senior positions and grounded at one time lost the brevet. Then a considerate head of department allowed cabin staff 'retiring' to uniformed catering jobs on the ground to keep their wings.

While the stewardess's job is not so attractive as it was 25 years ago, some of the sparkle remains. There is always the unexpected celebrity turning up on ordinary scheduled flights and special occasions when a plane is chartered to carry an orchestra, film unit, ballet company or an athletics team. The list of famous names passing through Heathrow airport every day is a lengthy one. It can include Cabinet ministers, film stars, pop groups, authors, tele-

vision personalities and other people in the news.

Occasionally, there is a royal flight. When Prince Philip flew from London to Malta in an Elizabethan on 26th November 1952, he was the first member of the Royal Family to fly BEA. The same aircraft flew him back six days later, calling at Rome en route to pick up the Duchess of Kent. Since then, almost every member of the Royal Family has flown with the corporation in turbo-prop aircraft and jets. Specially chartered aircraft are used for state visits and other official occasions, but some royal flights are now taken informally on ordinary scheduled services.

Special crockery and cutlery are provided for the official

In from Nice: The Supremes

flights by the Queen and her family. The passenger cabin of the plane is turned into a stateroom with special chairs and tables. BEA also provides the meals for the Queen's Flight of the Royal Air Force and its services within Europe, the eastern Mediterranean and North Africa. There is an average of 15 trips a month by aircraft of the Queen's Flight.

First-class passengers flying with BEA are given Sovereign Service, the airline's own name for special treatment. The first-class passengers get free drinks, bigger and more comfortable seats which are two abreast and have more leg room. As there are only a dozen or 16 first-class seats, these passengers can be given greater attention by the senior stewardess. The ratio of stewardesses to passengers in tourist class might be as little as one to fifty.

First-class seats are usually placed at the front of the aircraft, farthest from the engines. First-class passengers are taken separately when coaches are needed to move passengers across the tarmac aprons to the planes. They are taken on board last of all so that there is a minimum of waiting, and are first to disembark. The choice of food is more varied and every extra is provided. But first-class fares are often double the price of an economy ticket.

Paying the extra made all the difference before 1953 when hot meals were introduced. Tourist class passengers were given sandwiches. De luxe catering was provided on

141

The Duke of Edinburgh takes over the controls of a Trident (1964)

Right: Yuri Gagarin compares the Viscount with the Vostok I

'Silver Wing' services to Paris and Lisbon, and the 'Ulster Flyer' to Belfast. First-class passengers on 'Clansman' flights to Glasgow even got steaming Scots porridge. These superior services were possible because of the introduction of Elizabethans and Viscounts with pressurised cabins. But there were those who said, and still say, that no matter how good the food is, pressurised cabins blunt the senses of taste and smell. BEA did not stop trying to tickle the palate of the gournets, however. In February 1967, Col-chester oysters—three each—were served with caviar and champagne to Sovereign Service passengers on London–Paris flights. BEA gives VIPs extra special treatment and also has a category known as CIPs—Commercially Important Passengers—who are looked after with great care. But service can be no better than first class and when the trimmings are swept aside, all the passengers want the same thing—to be flown to their destination on time in safety and comfort.

The original Board of Directors of BEA in 1947 before Sir Harold Hartley and Mr Whitney Straight had left. From the left: Mr Walter Edmenson, Mr Whitney Straight, Mr Gerard d'Erlanger, Sir Harold Hartley, Mr. I. J. Hayward, Sir Patrick Dollan and Wing Commander A. H. Measures. The photo was taken at Northolt

CHAPTER 9

FROM THE TOP

BRITISH EUROPEAN AIRWAYS started life as a sickly child, plagued by nearly every complaint an infant airline could get. It was unknown and given equipment which did not fit. It cost a lot to run and never looked·like earning its keep. It was overshadowed by 'big brother' BOAC and stood helpless when its twin—British South American Airways—died at the age of three.

Now BEA is 25 and healthy. The scars of its violent youth have disappeared; its growth has been both sustained and vigorous. But it did not grow big by accident, nor was progress inevitable. BEA was born a nationalised concern and it is highly unlikely that it could have survived such a prolonged bad start had it been a private company. But without a guiding hand it could have stumbled into oblivion soon after B.S.A.A.

The hand was that of Marshal of the Royal Air Force, Lord Douglas of Kirtleside, who took over on 14th March 1949. No man could have been more suitable for the position of chairman of BEA. His leadership was about to transform the fortunes of the airline. Sir Winston Churchill's premiership had shaped the destiny of Britain. For BEA, Lord Douglas was a Churchill in miniature. He was to stay in office for 15 years, longer than any chairman of any nationalised company before or since.

BEA's first chairman was Sir Harold Hartley, who had joined the London, Midland and Scottish Railway in 1930 and was made chairman of Railway Air Services in 1934. This led to the top job in the Associated Airways Joint Committee, a coalition of British internal airlines banded together during the war. It was logical that Sir Harold should get the job of starting up BEA, for it was planned from the beginning that the new airline would take over the domestic routes of the A.A.J.C. which included Railway Air Services.

Sir Harold had his first flight in 1916, when he was taken up to study the effectiveness of a smoke-screen he had invented. He was chemical adviser to the 3rd Army in France in 1915 and organised the gas defence of the British Expeditionary Force. After the first world war he returned to Oxford as a science tutor.

Sir Harold, a severely dressed Victorian figure, took on the chairmanship of BEA at 68 with experience of research, teaching, the Army, railways and commerce behind him. His deputy was Air Commodore Whitney Straight, a dashing young airman of 34. Mr Straight had had a meteoric rise to prominence. He flew solo at 16; won many international car races at Brooklands and other tracks; formed the Straight Corporation which controlled 21 companies operating airlines, flying clubs and aerodromes; fought as a fighter pilot in World War Two, was shot down, captured and escaped; became Air A.D.C. to King George VI, and had collected a string of decorations—all by the time he had reached 33.

The managing director was Mr Gerard 'Pops' d'Erlanger who had 15 years flying experience. He had joined the board of British Airways in 1935 and switched to BOAC in 1940 where he took charge of the Air Safety Committee. In 1938 he suggested to the Air Ministry that there were many experienced pilots, unfit for active services, who could carry out communications and ferry flights. A year later, he was asked to form the Air Transport Auxiliary which delivered 308,000 aircraft during the war. Mr d'Erlanger flew almost every type of military aircraft.

The directors included Wing Commander Arthur Measures, who had been actively interested in aviation since 1912 and flew in the first world war. He had worked with Imperial Airways and Railway Air Services. Mr Walter Edmenson had represented the Ministry of War Transport in Northern Ireland and arranged all the movements of the American troops in transit. Sir Patrick Dollan was chairman of the Scottish Advisory Council. He had been Lord Provost of Glasgow and had helped to get the Rolls Royce aero engine works established in Glasgow where 25,000 Merlin engines for Spitfires were produced. Mr I. J. Hayward had long experience of the trades union movement and of public service in local government.

The team had been chosen carefully. All branches of the new airline would be in the hands of specialists. But all too soon, the hand-picked combination of experts had been broken up. Eight months after BEA began, its chairman and deputy chairman had been posted to BOAC.

In his one Christmas message to the staff, Sir Harold said: 'I don't like the word "organisation". It sounds mechanical and soulless, and I want BEA to be a living organism. I want it to have the sensitive co-ordination of the parts of the living body, with their quick responses through the nerve fibres to tell us when action is needed or that all is not well.'

Mr J. V. Wood, who was Managing Director of BEA when this photograph was taken in August, 1947

Mr Peter Masefield, who joined BEA in January, 1949, as assistant to the Chairman

BEA was alive, but its responses were still sluggish. For it was soon clear that all was *not* well and action was urgently needed. With the quick departure of the top two, Mr d'Erlanger took over as chairman with Mr John Keeling (later knighted) coming in as deputy. The new managing director was Mr John Wood and the rest of the board remained the same.

Britain was heading for an economic crisis. With it came a cut in pleasure travel and a ban on allowances for holidays abroad. BEA's staff had grown to 7,800—an increase of over 2,000 in less than a year. Redundancies had to follow and the airline announced that one-third of its work force would be released. In the turmoil that followed, only 700 were declared redundant. More than 1,500 left of their own accord, but they were replaced and the total in March 1948 was 7,069. It was still too big. The new leaders had not been ruthless enough in their pruning. But they had been in office for less than a year.

What chance had they had to sort themselves out? How could they throw men out of work when the airline was still struggling to expand and other jobs were hard to come by?

Mr d'Erlanger wrote in December, 'A Christmas message should be full of good cheer and optimism. It should abound with mutual congratulations and generally emit an aura and, if possible, an odour of real Christmas festivity, of roast turkey and blazing Yuletide logs all well lubricated with suitable refreshment. I think you will agree, however, that such outpourings, under the circumstances in which we find ourselves, would hardly be apt. And so while skirting the gloom of the long shadows cast by the surrounding storm clouds I cannot venture too far out into the cheerful glare traditionally associated with a white Christmas.'

In his new job he had many critics. But if nothing else, he had earned a reputation for compassion. Soon after the airline was formed, the staff used to lunch together in the hall of Bourne School, the headquarters. One morning Mr d'Erlanger walked in unannounced and sat down in the nearest vacant seat. Turning to the junior next to him he asked:

'Got a decent job?'

Between spoonfuls the answer came back, 'Not so bad. What's yours?'

The chairman's modest reply gave no hint of his identity and the junior continued blissfully unaware.

Some of the arguments between BEA and Whitehall had been fiery. There were rows over aircraft, new routes and over the vast number of workers the airline had engaged. Mr Peter Masefield arrived in January 1949 as assistant to the chairman to find the situation worsening. In February, matters came to a head over a proposed new service linking North and South Wales. The Minister of Civil Aviation, Lord Pakenham (now Lord Longford), announced the new route. Mr d'Erlanger opposed it, contesting that it could never run at a profit and that BEA

was already limited to the losses it could incur. By the 28th of the month, Mr d'Erlanger—then aged 43—had been sacked from his £6,500-a-year job. He was to continue in aviation and later received a knighthood. He died in 1962. Less than five months after the chairman's departure, managing director John Wood had resigned. His health had been poor, but it was obvious that he disagreed with the long-term plans for BEA and felt that the Civil Air Ministry had been taking too active a part in the management of the state-owned airline. Tragically, he died soon afterwards in an air crash on his way to a new job in Brazil. He was 45.

Lord Douglas had arrived and before the end of the year had made Peter Masefield his chief executive. Mr Masefield was 35 and he loved aeroplanes. He had been taken to the 1929 Aero Show at Olympia (an indoor affair like today's motor show) and as a 15-year-old schoolboy was able to see and touch the shiny new planes. The smell of the aeroplane dope and the magic of the new sport captivated him. By 1942 he was personal adviser on civil aviation to the Lord Privy Seal and secretary of the War Cabinet Committee on Air Transport. Mr Edward Heath, the Prime Minister, was still a young politician out for experience and for a year he acted as Mr Masefield's assistant. For two years Mr Masefield was director of long-term planning and projects at the Civil Aviation Ministry. Then he was asked to join BEA.

Here is how he saw the situation when he arrived:

'BEA was losing money hand over fist and had rock-bottom morale. We had to have a redundancy of over 1,000 when I first came in. This was one of the toughest things I had to do, one of the first things I did. As a new broom it was easier.

'Pops' d'Erlanger thought that paperwork was the right answer. One of the first things he gave me with great pride was Standing Orders, two volumes literally eight inches thick. You couldn't do a thing without looking at these Standing Orders. I ceremoniously put them on the fire.

'Sholto, Lord Douglas, came in March. We always got on absolutely fine, no problems. In fact, I always look on my chief executiveship and his chairmanship as one of the ideal relationships. We really worked hand in glove. I liked him very much and I think he liked me. We always maintained, right to his death, a very close relationship. We never had a cross word.

'The rest of the staff were suspicious of him to begin with because here was an Air Marshal coming in to tell them how to do things and they hadn't realised that Sholto had been in civil aviation before some of them were born. The way we worked was he looked after ministers and I looked after running the airline.

'We had five jobs to do. We had to get the morale right and one of the first things was to stop the fight between Tony Milward and G. O. 'Joe' Waters. [Managers respectively of the Continental and English divisions.] So I knocked their heads together. Then we had to get the organisation right, to get an aircraft programme, a better route structure and finally to achieve profits at the first possible moment.'

BEA made its first profit in 1955 and soon afterwards Mr Masefield left to become chairman of Bristol Aircraft Limited. Today he is chairman of the British Airports Authority, the state-owned concern which runs Heathrow, Gatwick, Stansted and Prestwick airports. He had accepted the challenge of putting BEA on its feet with vigour and his enthusiasm had been infectious. He boosted the staff and won a reputation for putting out propaganda slogans. His sayings were amusing and encouraging; there was one for almost every department.

He had flown almost every type of aircraft used by the airline and was able to sit down with pilots to discuss their problems, using his own flying experience to good advantage. He had kept everyone aware of BEA's plans and progress by writing full accounts in the staff magazine. Even the annual report took on a new look as Mr Masefield packed it with charts, diagrams, maps and pictures to illustrate his points.

The chief executive had been with BEA for nearly seven years. As he was leaving, the airline was about to announce its plans for the Vanguard. Details of the new plane and even its name were closely guarded secrets until the official announcement on 17th October 1955. But Mr Masefield could not resist a reference to a 'great new aeroplane' in the staff magazine which appeared 11 days before the official statement. And impishly he added: 'It will, I believe, be as much in the vanguard of its contemporaries as was the Viscount.'

There were two reasons why he left.

'We'd got the best equipped airline in Europe,' he said, 'profitable with a good route structure and an organisation which ticked. So the major challenge had come out of it.

'Secondly, I'd got four children all of whom were coming up to the expensive educational stage. As chief executive I had cut my own salary by £2,000 a year soon after arriving and I had come to the point where I couldn't put it up though it hadn't grown. I think I was then getting about £4,500 a year. When I was offered £12,000 to go to Bristol and return to my first love of aircraft manufacture it was more than I could withstand. But I decided to change with great regret, I didn't really want to go. In all the years I've been in aviation I think I enjoyed most those seven years with BEA. We were achieving things all the time. We had a jolly good team.'

There had been no doubt that Mr Masefield was allowed to get on with his work because of the protection against Whitehall interference given to him by the dominant figure of Lord Douglas. An impressive career in aviation over 30 years, together with experience of dealing with politicians, made him uniquely suited to the job of chairman of BEA. He took over from a man who had been sacked for not co-operating and immediately jolted the Government by his stubborn refusal to let ministers interfere.

Civil aviation was in its infancy in May 1919 when a British commercial pilot's licence, the fourth in existence, was issued to 25-year-old William Sholto Douglas. He had won the Military Cross, Distinguished Flying Cross and Croix de Guerre in combat as a Royal Flying Corps fighter pilot. For a year after the first world war he flew as an airline captain with Handley Page Transport Ltd on the London–Paris and Brussels routes. Sometimes he would look down from the open cockpit of his Handley Page 0/400 and see the buses on the Edgware Road overtaking him!

He returned to a service career by joining the Royal Air Force, rising to Air Marshal and deputy Chief of Air Staff by 1939. At various stages of the war he was in charge of Fighter, Coastal and Middle East Commands. Afterwards he took charge of Britain's military forces in Germany and then became Military Governor of the British Military Zone of Germany. The legend of his leadership had been cast. One of his colleagues said: 'Sholto just assumes absolute power when he takes his seat. It makes it impossible for anyone to defy him.'

Lord Douglas was a socialist, but this did not confine his principle that BEA—a state-owned corporation—could and must pay its way. All but two of his 15 years in office were to be under Conservative Governments, but it did not alter his attitude towards Whitehall. In dealing with nine successive ministers responsible for aviation, Lord Douglas was determined to keep politics from interfering with the airline in general, and in particular with Mr Masefield and later Sir Anthony Milward, his two chief executives.

While these two right-hand men piloted themselves around Britain and Europe in BEA planes, Lord Douglas chose to be flown and took every opportunity on short trips to publicise the airline's helicopters. In 1955 his third wife, Hazel, decided she should learn to fly. Lady Douglas took instruction at Croydon aerodrome and her husband went to watch. He had not flown since 1947, but the sight of the tiny Auster Aiglet trainers was too much and he fixed himself a flight. After half an hour's dual instruction

he made a good landing, then went on to fly solo and at the age of 62 regained his pilot's licence.

There was no hint of retirement in 1959 when he was presented with a BEA buttonhole badge, awarded to all the staff after ten years' service. The airline was by this time hugely successful and although outwardly shy, Lord Douglas was obviously enjoying every minute of his new triumph and longevity of office. Douglas Bader, the legless Spitfire ace, who had served under his command during the war, snorted: 'Let those who delight in denigrating admirals, field-marshals and air marshals stick that in their pipes and smoke it!'

Despite his success, Lord Douglas stuck to his principles. He did not, for example, believe that being chairman of BEA automatically entitled him to first-class travel. Returning from Rome with his family in 1960 in the tourist section of the plane, he explained that the first-class seats had all been taken, saying: 'I put our names on the first-class list a month before, but there wasn't room for us. You can't displace people who have booked before you.'

One of his first battles was to get the Viscount for BEA. The plane had a string of faults. It was underpowered and too small. At first, Lord Douglas wavered. Then when its potential was outlined by the people he had appointed within BEA, he took on the task personally of pushing it to the front. Whitehall persisted in backing the Elizabethan and the 20-seat Handley Page Marathon. Face to face with the warrior from two wars, the opposition wilted. Lord Douglas would fix his keen blue eyes on an unfortunate minister's face, light his pipe and then softly but firmly put his case. Resisting him seemed to be a waste of time.

He fought hard, but lost, the battle for BEA to retain a monopoly of British passenger trunk routes. But he won the fight to keep BEA separate from BOAC despite pressure from all quarters, including BOAC itself. He also succeeded in steering the Government to back the Trident, the jet *he* wanted BEA to have. Despite his good relations

William Sholto Douglas in front of his S.E.5 during the First World War

Lord Douglas, revives his wartime memories by posing with an S.E.5a at Farnborough in 1959

with his former chief executive, Peter Masefield, who had joined the company producing the Trident's rival, Lord Douglas's beliefs had no room for the old pals' act.

There seemed to be no end to his energy. He was 63 when he became president of the International Air Transport Association, the clearing house for all agreements between the world's airlines. He was also a vice-president of the Football Association. When the time came for Lord Douglas to leave, one of his staff said: 'We shall have to get another chairman, but we will never find a replacement.'

Among the names rumoured for the post, worth £8,500 a year plus £1,000 expenses, were Air Chief Marshal Sir Edmund Hudleston and Marshal of the Royal Air Force Sir Thomas Pike. There was talk, too, that Mr Whitney Straight might be brought back.

Lord Douglas's departure was marked by an unusual gift from the staff of 17,000. The Government had allowed him to keep the eight-year-old Bentley he had used as chairman of BEA. He had mentioned casually in his office one day that his garage was too small for the car which was usually kept in one of BEA's garages after a chauffeur had driven him home. To his delight, the parting gift was a new garage—planned and built at the expense of BEA's employees.

Lord Douglas retired on 31st March 1964, 15 years and 17 days after being sent in to sort out a sick airline. He had done his job and more. BEA had been put on a sound footing and there was no longer any doubt about its survival. But the chairman was 70 and could have gone five years before. He had served five Governments and had gained the respect of them all. But no chairman of a nationalised company ever before lasted so long; most welcome a change after a few years in one job.

Peter Masefield explains: 'Sholto stayed because he wanted the best pension he could get. He married again; he'd got a young daughter who was the apple of his eye— he'd never had any children by two previous marriages. Sholto was very worried about his pension. Every year he

stayed at BEA put his pension up by about £1,000.'

After five peaceful years in retirement, Lord Douglas died at the age of 75 on 29th October 1969.

The appointment of Sir Anthony Milward as chairman came as a surprise. It represented a departure from the Government's usual practice. The new chief was the first chairman of a nationalised industry to be appointed from within the same organisation. There were other shocks, too, for it was decided that BEA and BOAC ought to work closer together. At the time, this move was seen by many as the first step in a merger. Sir Anthony was made a part-time member of BOAC's board. Sir Giles Guthrie had already been on the board of BEA for five years when he was appointed chairman of BOAC in 1964. He stayed for five years and left both corporations in 1968.

Sir Anthony Milward had first flown in 1927 when he paid 5s (25p) for a joy-ride in an Avro 504K. He ignored the family firm in Redditch, Worcestershire, which made needles and joined a textile company in Manchester. He learned to fly with the Civil Air Guard in 1938 and spent $5\frac{1}{2}$ years in the Fleet Air Arm during the war, shunning desk jobs and spending all his time on flying duties. He relinquished three directorships to join BOAC after the war, but he had wanted to join Railway Air Services and when BEA took it over, he asked for a transfer to the new airline.

'It was a challenge,' he said. 'Nobody knew anything about short-haul European services. Sir Harold Hartley offered me £700 a year as general services manager—a subject about which I knew very little, property and that sort of thing. Sir Harold is a marvellous man. He was still writing to me about the accounts in 1970 when he was 94!'

Within a year of joining BEA, Sir Anthony had been put in charge of the continental division. There was no mistaking his jutting jaw, stiff brush of greying hair and cheerful determination. Power struggles rocked the airline and Sir Anthony was soon vying with G.O. 'Joe' Waters for a senior position. Sir Anthony lost the battle, but continued to be his modest if aggressive self. He had risen above his rival when Mr Masefield left, but Lord Douglas took his time appointing a new chief executive; he combined the job with his own for six months before inviting Sir Anthony on to the board in 1956. The new partnership stayed together for eight years until Lord Douglas's retirement. Both men tempered aggression with tact and became friends despite being poles apart politically.

'He was a very good chairman in every sense,' said Sir Anthony. 'Everyone trusted him. He was forthright, able, with a very good brain. He had the confidence of people around him. I worked for him for 15 years and I don't think we ever quarrelled. He looked after the politicians and he would say, "*You* are running the airline." Sometimes he did not agree with a proposal and would say quietly, "I think it is wrong, but if you want to do it this way, do it. But just think." I tried to do the same with Henry Marking when I was chairman.

'Sholto was a contradiction in dozens of different ways, but he got on well with the rest of the staff. I think nearly everybody trusted him. But if you are running a nationalised industry you have to be extremely tough because politicians and civil servants will walk over you if you will possibly let them. You have to say "I'm sorry, I am running this business, and not you." You won't always defy them and being chairman of a nationalised industry is one of the most insecure jobs in the world. I stayed for so long, I think, by being tough and knowing my mind. I have always taken the view, and I'm sure Sholto did, that if you knew your mind and stated it clearly you would get on. I very seldom had a row with any politician or civil servant.

'Back in the forties it looked very doubtful to me and to many of us as to whether we could ever make money. The thing which changed the whole aspect of BEA was the arrival of the Viscount. This was Sholto's greatest achievement. Peter Masefield's too. When they arrived we had just turned down the Viscount and had bought the Elizabethan.

'Then there was the most fearful row when Sholto went off to the Ministry of Civil Aviation and said he wasn't going to buy the Marathon which had been built for us. We sat down again and thought the whole problem of new aircraft through with our engineers and the result was the Viscount. Rolls Royce found they could produce a lot more power from the Dart engines. The plane put us on the map immediately.'

The Viscount was tailor-made for BEA and is one of the biggest success stories in British aviation. But other planes built specifically for BEA, notably the Vanguard and Trident, have not sold well elsewhere.

'This is a thing which always makes me cross,' said Sir Anthony. 'It needs a lot of examination. Boeing got the idea of a three-engined aircraft from the Trident. We had a two-year start, but by the time we had got our first five Tridents, Boeing had produced something like a hundred 727s. Having started off two years behind they could see the Trident was too small. It was no fault of BEA's. We bought the aircraft we wanted and we were running the airline. People would say, "Do you think it is right to have a tailor-made aircraft?" And I would say, "Of course I do. It must be."

'To use this analogy further, if you say to your tailor you want a suit and he measures you up and asks seventy guineas, you might say you couldn't possibly afford it. He then says he could make it cheaper off the peg, but you are being asked to buy a suit which does not fit. Hawker Siddeley were very pleased to have the initial Trident order and all this business about not selling came up later. We had exactly the same problem with Rolls Royce, who said they did not want to make the Spey engine for the Trident because it wasn't big enough. This gave us a real laugh because the Spey engine is worth thinking about now with poor old Rolls' troubles. The Spey engine was the biggest money-spinner, I think, they ever had and it would not have been built for the Trident had it not been for BEA.

Sir Anthony Milward, who became Chairman of BEA in 1964

We had to bully them into doing it. This question never ceases to rile me.'

Sir Anthony was taken off the top of the pack to become chairman of BEA in 1964. He had hoped for the appointment and even expected it, but there was no way of being sure. He promoted Mr Henry Marking, then secretary of BEA, to chief executive. Of his own promotion, he said: 'I was very pleased about it, naturally. I am equally pleased about the appointment of Henry Marking who succeeded me because I think a top of the pack appointment is good for morale. It shows there is nothing to stop anyone becoming chairman. It is a Government appointment, but with a very strong recommendation from the retiring chairman. When I took over I wanted to go my own way although I acknowledged the very successful way Lord Douglas had done things. I wanted to know much more about the details than he did. I think I delegated powers—I hope I did—and was more active. Sholto said to me after I'd been made chief executive and was having my first talk with him, "Well, Tony, I want you to know that I am naturally a lazy man. You are the chap who is going to do all the work." He was quite honest and he said it with a smile and he worked that way. I liked to think that until I retired I did know jolly well what was going on all over the corporation.'

Sir Anthony retired at the age of 66 in 1970. He had been on the board for more than 14 years, the last six as chairman. He took over in a year when a record profit of £3 million had been announced. He left in a year when the figure was over £6½ million.

Mr Marking became the fifth chairman of BEA on 1st January 1971. Unlike all the chairmen and chief executives that had gone before him, he had had no interest in aviation until he came to BEA, and he was not a pilot. He joined BEA as assistant solicitor in 1949. But first he had made sure that his old firm in Tunbridge Wells, where he had been in private practice, would take him back if the temporary job with the airline did not work out.

He had no regrets at leaving the safe, respectable but boring life of a country solicitor. He became secretary of the airline in 1950 and spent the next 14 years learning the business, mainly from Lord Douglas whom he found 'an absolutely marvellous person to work for and work with.'

'I think at the start he tried you out and if he thought you were a doormat he would walk on you,' said Mr Marking. 'But if he realised you were not a doormat he would treat you very kindly. He could not have been kinder or more helpful to me and I learned an enormous amount from him. In certain circumstances I still think to myself, "Now what would Sholto have done?" and that's not a bad guide.'

The full story of BEA's first 25 years is reflected in the following table:

1947	£2,157,937	loss	1959	£232,695	profit
1948	£3,573,989	loss	1960	£2,086,078	profit
1949	£2,763,085	loss	1961	£1,545,321	profit
1950	£1,363,594	loss	1962	£1,488,065	loss
1951	£979,267	loss	1963	£265,301	loss
1952	£1,423,611	loss	1964	£3,030,007	profit
1953	£1,459,131	loss	1965	£1,316,876	profit
1954	£1,773,797	loss	1966	£1,283,725	profit
1955	£63,039	profit	1967	£708,296	profit
1956	£603,614	profit	1968	£1,784,000	loss
1957	£216,770	profit	1969	£3,536,000	profit
1958	£1,054,807	profit	1970	£6,532,000	profit

Mr Marking was 29 when he came to BEA; he was willing to learn from anyone. Of Peter Masefield, he said, 'He was a splendid person to work for, firstly because he wasn't particularly interested in my side of the work, so he did not try to interfere. Secondly, he had a wonderful knack, which no doubt he still has, of making you feel that what you were doing was important. That made life much more fun and much more interesting.'

Having been made chief executive in 1964, Mr Marking

Mr. Henry Marking, the fifth, and present Chairman of BEA

was given the top job at the age of 50. Sir Anthony Milward said, 'I had a private fear that we might have been asked to accept someone unknown to the industry and ourselves from outside. But we have someone known to us all.'

The changes meant that since 1949 the airline has had only four men in its top two positions. They have been Douglas–Masefield (1949–55); Douglas–Milward (1956–64); Milward–Marking (1964–70); Marking (1971). Mr Marking began by combining the posts of chairman and chief executive with former chief engineer Mr Kenneth Wilkinson as deputy chief executive.

There have been remarkably few changes on the board of the airline in its first 25 years. It has had only three deputy chairman. Mr Straight served for eight months and was replaced by Sir John Keeling who stayed for more than 18 years. He was followed by the present deputy, Sir Kenneth Keith.

The top ten members in terms of length of service on the board are:

1	Mr Aubrey Ping	1/9/49 to 31/3/70	20 years 212 days
2	Sir John Keeling	24/7/47 to 30/9/65	18 years 68 days
3	Sir Walter Edmenson	16/12/46 to 15/12/63	17 years
4	Mr S. Kenneth Davies	12/3/51 to 11/3/67	16 years
5	Lord Douglas of Kirtleside	14/3/49 to 31/3/64	15 years 17 days
6	Sir Anthony Milward	3/5/56 to 31/12/70	14 years 242 days
7	Sir Patrick Dollan	28/11/46 to 15/12/63	13 years 185 days
8	Lord Balfour of Inchrye	1/7/55 to 30/6/66	11 years
9	Sir Giles Guthrie	1/4/59 to 31/12/68	9 years 275 days
10	Sir Arnold Overton	19/11/53 to 8/1/63	9 years 51 days

There have been many others with long records of service with BEA. Captain J. W. G. James joined the board in December 1964 after being flight operations director and chief pilot since 1946. Mr Kenneth Wilkinson, who became managing director and deputy chief executive in 1971, has also been with the airline since it began. So too have Mr John Guy, Mr Cyril Herring, Mr Philip Lawton, Mr Robert McKean and Mr Ian Scott-Hill. They are at the same time old hands and new leaders.

CHAPTER 10

WILL HELICOPTERS SURVIVE?

THE BIG SIKORSKY S61N roars up into the teeth of the gale and bucks out over the coast 500 feet above the foaming sea. The landing pad on the mainland at Aberdeen shrivels to the size of a sixpence as the helicopter pilot sets his course. His destination is not even a dot on an ordinary map—it is an oil drilling rig 150 miles out through the worst of a North Sea storm. Ninety minutes later the rig is spotted, standing clear of the heaving sea on massive steel legs. It is the only feature in miles of grey water. The platform is high above the waves but the wind rips across it in unchecked fury.

The pilot chews his gum more quickly now, hands gripping the controls as the twin turbine engines, each producing 1,350 horse power, pound away. The helicopter scythes past the rig and wheels into the buffeting wind, coming cautiously to the landing platform which looks to be the size of a postage stamp. Anti-skid paint and de-icer fluid have been sprayed over the surface. But a small error could send the $8\frac{1}{2}$-ton aircraft smashing into the derrick towering beside the platform, or plunging into the turbulent sea. The helicopter is fitted with floats and is amphibious. But it would last only minutes in the gale and its crew would perish in seconds in the icy water.

This kind of flying is some of the most dangerous taken on anywhere in the world. But BEA pilots have harnessed the wild weather which is encountered on daily flights to the growing forest of drilling rigs probing for oil and gas off Britain's east coast.

The powerful Sikorskys, capable of carrying 24 passengers, have been ferrying men, mail, medicine and food to the rigs from Beccles, Lowestoft and Aberdeen for the past six years. They were chosen because of their size, range and twin engines. They can get back to base for repairs from a rig even if one power unit fails. The fleet is under contract to the oil companies 24 hours a day and apart from routine flights, pilots are always standing by for rescue operations. Without this kind of support, the drilling firms would have great difficulty in finding men to work on these isolated platforms. It was a BEA S61N which saved the crew of the rig *Sea Quest* which broke loose in a force ten gale 110 miles off Flamborough Head in January 1968.

BEA's fleet of S61N helicopters often flies as many as 250 hours a month from Aberdeen and 150 from Suffolk. The difference in these totals is because the rigs are a three-hour return flight from Aberdeen and only an hour's return journey from the two Suffolk bases. On many mornings the helicopters are completely covered in ice.

157

Continued on page 163

Above: BEA Bell 4-7J helicopter in flight (1959)

Left: BEA S-51 helicopter leaving Northolt for Heathrow (1951)

Below: Bell 47 B3 helicopter with crop spraying boom (1959)

159

Above: Westland Sikorsky WS-55 leaving Battersea
Heliport (1959). Below: the WS-55 fitted with floats

Left: Sikorsky S-61N inaugurates the Penzance to Scilly helicopter service (1964)

Above: A BEA Bell Jet Ranger helicopter fitted with skis (1970)

Continued from page 157

Engineers spend up to half an hour carefully chipping it from the controls and rotors. Flying conditions sometimes mean a mixture of fog, gales, snow and ice. Everyone on the rigs is exposed to the full blast of what is known on the East Coast as the 'lazy' wind. New pilots soon learn that this is a wind which cannot be bothered to go around, it just bites straight through!

At the other side of the country there is another group of lonely outposts whose inhabitants are equally pleased when a BEA Sikorsky arrives. These are the Scilly Isles where traders rely on a fast, regular connection to the mainland. The Penzance-Scilly Isles link has been operated by the 24-seat helicopters ever since the retirement of the eight-seat Dragon Rapides. More than 58,000 passengers a year travel on the one S61N, which has no replacement standing by. It is a tribute to the aircraft's reliability that a service can be run without a back-up helicopter. The Sikorsky completes 98 per cent of its scheduled services in a year and it is seldom more than five minutes overdue.

The 35-mile crossing used to begin at Land's End, but

in 1964 the mainland base was moved to a new heliport at Penzance, the first to be built and operated by an airline in this country and the first in Europe to combine both terminal and maintenance facilities. The service is the only vertical take-off and landing (VTOL) scheduled operation available to the public in Britain.

This aerial bridge and the North Sea flights are the only regular features in the work of BEA Helicopters Ltd, a subsidiary entirely owned by the parent corporation. The company has 28 pilots in a staff of 160 based at Gatwick, Penzance and Lowestoft and runs a fleet of five Sikorsky S61Ns plus a four-passenger Agusta-Bell 206 JetRanger. The JetRanger is a nippy executive aircraft available for charter throughout the year. It was hired by party leaders in the last General Election, but at £85 an hour, it is as well to be sure that your journey is really necessary.

The best feature about the subsidiary is that after years of experimentation which was a steady drain on resources, BEA Helicopters is now making money. A profit of £40,000 was recorded in 1970 and BEA chairman Henry Marking commented: 'Helicopters have been waiting in the wings pretty expensively and I am very glad to see that the helicopter company is paying its way after all these years.'

BEA began with helicopters in 1947 when three Sikorsky S-51 and two Bell 47B-3 aircraft were ordered from America for its Helicopter Experimental Unit at Yeovil, Somerset. The airline had short routes and knew it could not afford to miss out if this form of transport could be made to pay. But the gap between the cost of providing a seat in a helicopter and a seat in a plane was wide even in 1947 when the largest aeroplanes were carrying fewer than 50 people. Today, the modern jets with 150 passengers can provide seats at a quarter of the price of one in a helicopter.

The pilots of the Experimental Unit scratched around for a purpose in 1947. There were no oil rigs to serve and their aircraft could not carry as many passengers as a Dragon Rapide. The obvious answer seemed to be to make full use of the helicopter's ability to lift off from a small base. If the landing pad could be in the centre of a town, it would be much more convenient and quicker for passengers than going out to a conventional airport several miles away. In theory, it makes sense to fly from small patches of grass instead of vast concrete runways. But the helicopter's hopes end there. It cannot be run as cheaply as one of the large modern planes. It is limited for technical reasons to speeds of 160 mph. The addition of a stub wing, making it a compound helicopter, allows speeds up to 250 mph. The complexity of the mechanical parts means that much more maintenance is needed than for a fixed-wing aircraft. The rotors are perfect for lifting the helicopter into the air but far less efficient for forward flight. Despite the ruggedness of the S61Ns on flights to the oil rigs, helicopters are vulnerable in bad weather, particularly high winds.

As if all this were not enough, authorities continue to frown on the helicopter as a link between city centres because of the noise it makes and the safety factor. Single-engine machines are not usually allowed over built-up areas and those flying over London follow the path of the river Thames or go North and South over a main railway line. Such restrictions smack of the times when men with red flags had to walk in front of motor-cars and trains.

BEA has been reluctant to invest money in the development of helicopters, but it has made repeated attempts to operate them like fixed-wing aircraft on scheduled services. A real purpose for the Sikorsky S-51s and Bell 47s seemed to have been found in January 1948 when dummy runs to investigate the possibility of carry mail were made in the West Country by the Experimental Unit. A Sikorsky S-51 went round a 115-mile route from Yeovil to Sherborne, Gillingham, Blandford, Wimborne, Poole, Wareham, Dorchester, Weymouth, Bridgeport, Lyme Regis and back to Yeovil in less than two hours. One of the Bell 47s flew over a 22-mile route serving villages north-east of Yeovil.

In the following months, regular mail runs were made between Stornoway and Inverness, Glasgow and Islay, and Stornoway and Glasgow.

On 1st June 1948 BEA started the first helicopter-operated public mail service in Britain from Peterborough to a dozen points in East Anglia. The route had been chosen carefully, as Peterborough was on the main railway line between London and the North. In addition, it was difficult to journey east by public transport from Peterborough. The Deputy Mayor of the city presented a Royal Air Mail pennant to BEA's Captain Theilmann, who took off on a route covering King's Lynn, Wells, Sheringham, Cromer, Norwich, Thetford, Diss, Harleston, Great Yarmouth, Lowestoft, Beccles and East Dereham. The S-51s continued to hop round these stepping stones until September when the route was abandoned because of the cost. More than 30,000 lbs of mail was carried, 95 per cent of the scheduled flights had been completed and bad weather prevented only a few of the stops being ruled out. But at £28 4s (£28·20) an hour it was too expensive. BEA's next move was a night mail service. Parcels and letters which could be moved at a time when no other means of transport was available might make money. But once again, practice disproved the theory.

There was real hope when the world's first regular scheduled passenger service by helicopters was started by BEA on a June morning in 1950. The three S-51s had been named after Round Table knights Sir Baudwin, Sir Owen and Sir Lamorak. A fourth S-51 crashed at Croesor Dam, Merioneth before it had received the accolade. It was given a string of unofficial names by the pilot, who calmly retrieved his coat from the wreckage and walked off. The new service ran from Liverpool to Cardiff with an optional stop at Plas Coch Farm, Wrexham. But the S-51s could carry only three passengers at a time and BEA could not attract enough people to make the service pay. It was abandoned after ten months. A total of 819 passengers was carried.

Helicopter positioning a tower beacon near Gatwick Airport

Dummy run for the world's first helicopter mail service
(1948). It was hoped that the BEA S-51 would speed up
mail transit, but the scheme was not a success and was abandoned

An S-61N Helicopter landing on the Thames near Fulham

Undismayed, BEA began a helicopter link from London airport, via Northolt, to Haymills Rotorstation 3½ miles from the centre of Birmingham in June 1951. Bad weather forced the first passenger carrying flight to be diverted to Thame, Oxfordshire. Lack of business brought a change of plan. The same route would be flown, this time as a freight service. Then two Bristol 171 helicopters were bought and 'knighted' instantly. They helped explore the possibility of linking the South Bank at Waterloo with the two main airports West of London. But all these experiments failed because the services lost money at alarming rates. Floods near Eindhoven, Holland, in February 1953 cost many lives. But the Sikorskys went into action and in five days two BEA pilots rescued 76 people, carried 44

The S-61N takes the strain at Battersea (1965)

anything, it was too fast for the passengers. From 800 feet above the curving path of the Thames they could see everything—providing they were quick enough in scrambling across from one side of the cabin to the other. Famous landmarks floated by and the chimneypots of London gave familiar places a new look. But there was no mistaking Buckingham Palace, Hampton Court and Richmond Hill. In ten months a total of 3,822 sightseers went on the 20-minute flight, but it was little more than a novelty which was bound to wear off.

BEA's chief executive Peter Masefield said plainly in 1954 that helicopters were 'small, slow, rather noisy and pretty expensive'. But he forecast that by 1957 it would cost £14 for a helicopter flight between London and Birmingham compared with a first-class rail fare of £1 4s 5d. By the early 1960s it would cost only £3 by helicopter and take 40 minutes instead of a two-hour train journey, he added. Fifty-seaters would be opening up on a big scale by 1964, cruising at 150 mph and costing 6d a mile per passenger. Vertical take-off aircraft would probably enter commercial services in 1969, Mr Masefield went on, but helicopters would have had a good run before they were outdated. In the meantime BEA would be extending

doctors and engineers, ferried medical stores, drinking water and food to villages cut off by the rising waters. The helicopter had at last proved its worth and many more mercy missions were to be flown by BEA's pilots in the years that followed.

The secret of a profitable scheduled service continued to elude BEA, however. Bristol 171s started a tie-up between London airport and Southampton for 50s (£2·50) return. The Westland-Sikorsky WS-55, cruising at 75 mph and carrying seven passengers, was brought in for a regular run between Heathrow and Waterloo in July 1955. If

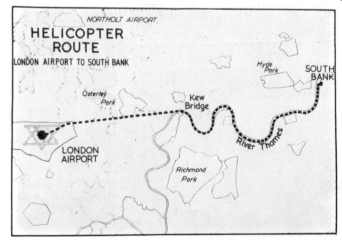

The helicopter shuttle between Heathrow and central London

Strong turbulence in the North Wales mountains brought down this Sikorsky helicopter in 1949. No-one was injured. Afterwards the pilot, Captain Dennis Bryan, went back to rescue his jacket . . .

its existing routes and in 1958 it would start a London–Brussels service. Needless to say, Mr Masefield's predictions were wildly optimistic. BEA was still studying, no more than that, the possibility of using 250 mph compound helicopters carrying 86 passengers on routes from London to Paris, Brussels and Amsterdam in 1971.

By 1956, Mr Masefield had a renewed interest in the fortunes of the helicopter. He was then chairman of Bristol Aircraft Company, makers of the Bristol 173, which had a long body like a dachshund, a rotor at each end and five large windows on either side of the fuselage. Four separate wheels, which looked like the castors on a single bed, made up the undercarriage. The second prototype was painted in BEA colours and landed in a field next to the airline's headquarters at Ruislip. It was the first delivery of a twin-engined helicopter to any airline in the world. But the Bristol 173 never carried passengers for BEA and was abandoned after a series of experiments.

Scheduled runs around Birmingham, Leicester and Nottingham sprang up in 1956, but 1,829 passengers in four months were not enough to make the Midlands service pay. No opportunity was missed to promote the WS-55. Lord Douglas was photographed stepping from one when the new Westland Heliport on the South bank of the Thames at Battersea was opened in 1959. This was the image BEA wanted to put forward—top businessmen and helicopters. But the only thing that anyone seemed to notice was the noble Lord's striped socks!

No scheduled services were run by helicopter between November 1956 and May 1964. But BEA's fleet was often chartered for special flights. Business executives, VIPs, press and television were carried. It was as if the airline was inviting suggestions as to how it could best use its rotary-winged fleet. In the meantime the aircraft pulled stranded motorists out of snowdrifts, hoisted machinery in and out of inaccessible places, carried out aerial crane work and, on one occasion, helped in a search for a lost dog.

After eight years without a regular route, BEA had the first two of its Sikorsky S61Ns shipped across the Atlantic, assembled on the dockside at Southampton and flown to Gatwick. From there they were transferred to Cornwall to take over the Scilly Isles run.

In 24 years, BEA has operated 19 helicopters:

Sikorsky S-51 (four)
Bell 47B-3 (two)
Agusta-Bell 47J (one)
Bristol 171 Mk. 3A Sycamore (three)
Westland-Sikorsky WS-55 (three)
Sikorsky S61N (five)
Agusta-Bell 206A JetRanger (one)

The Fairey Rotodyne, part helicopter part fixed-wing aeroplane, might have been the realisation of Mr Masefield's dream had it not been so noisy and costly to run. Carrying 48 passengers at 165 mph over distances of 400 miles was ideal for flights within Britain; there is no doubt that the Rotodyne would have revolutionised inter-city travel.

BEA's experimental helicopter unit was replaced by the existing subsidiary company in 1964. The helicopters lost their titles when the tradition of naming individual aircraft was abandoned. It was just as well. Apart from the route in the West country, the noble 'knights' were impoverished odd-job men, servants at anyone's beck and call. Sometimes they were used for crop-spraying or traffic patrols above motorways.

One of the S61Ns landed heavy equipment on board the giant tanker *Torrey Canyon* which went aground on Seven Stones Reef near the Scilly Isles in March 1967. The helicopter carried in compressors with which it was hoped to pump out the stricken ship. A high degree of skill was needed to put the swaying equipment down on a ship which had no proper landing platform. Later, the tanker was bombed and burned in an attempt to prevent the oil polluting local beaches. The disaster cut the number of holidaymakers in Cornwall the following summer and this

Meals on the ground for traffic-jammed passengers (with acknowledgements to 'Punch', February, 1958)

was reflected in the numbers carried by BEA's helicopters from Penzance.

The JetRanger is the most modern helicopter in the fleet and has been a good advertisement for BEA. It has provided an air ambulance service during the Isle of Man's TT races and whisked chairmen into and out of air shows.

But the full potential of the helicopter for commercial flying has never been realised. If an airline like BEA, with such short distances between the major cities it serves, cannot use them profitably for inter-city travel then it is unlikely that anyone else can. The people who work at BEA's Ruislip headquarters are constantly reminded that they are in the flying business by the aircraft which swoop 40 feet above their flat-roofed offices to land at Northolt. You can look straight down the main runway from the chairman's suite of offices—an unsuspecting visitor ducks involuntarily as a plane roars off the tarmac and heads straight at the building.

But there is no such reminder about helicopters. When chairmen and chief executives are next stuck in a traffic jam on the M4 motorway, they might reflect that it would be so easy to connect Heathrow airport, not to mention BEA's Ruislip HQ, with West London Air Terminal. It is simply a question of providing landing pads and getting permission. The airline may never attempt such a service. But it has not forgotten the helicopter which, despite its fits and starts over the past 25 years, could still be the shape of airliners to come.

CHAPTER 11

BY 1996

BEA WILL BE 50 years of age in 1996. By that time the hundred or so aircraft it now owns, including the latest of its Trident Three fleet, will have been phased out. The airline celebrates its 25th anniversary in a strong position, but will it survive, and should it still be here, for a Golden Jubilee? Will it still be running internal services at a loss? Will it continue to serve only Europe and merely touch the hems of two other continents as it does today? Can it expand? Will there still be a 'toyshop' for helicopters?

Peter Masefield, older and wiser since his predictions on helicopters in 1954, is now chairman of the British Airports Authority and in a unique position to judge BEA's future. He believes there should be three main airlines in Britain and says:

'Basically, there should be a European airline which also has tentacles going out to feed in traffic from places like North America and Africa. There should be a round-the-world airline which has all the trimmings and could pick up traffic in Europe: that would be BOAC. Then there should be a third, based at Gatwick like Caledonian//BUA, serving South America, West Africa and going through central America and the Caribbean and central America to Australia. BEA and Caledonian//BUA should be allowed to fly the North Atlantic like Pan-American

Airways and TWA do—the route is fat enough. And BOAC should fly to Paris alongside BEA.

'Now that would be three very strong British airlines all in a certain amount of rivalry which is good, but each with its own sphere of influence and big enough to have a good business. They should have mixed economies, state ownership of 51 per cent with 49 per cent held on the

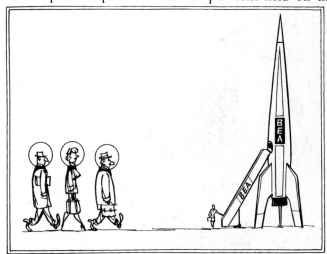

One cartoonist's idea of things to come

Stock Exchange so that you get the best of both worlds. But if it did happen, it would take thirty years.'

Chairman Henry Marking says BEA should remain separate from BOAC. He points out that BEA's long-term planning does not go up to 1996, but he adds: 'We have been keeping on with helicopters in the hope that one day there will be an economic VTOL aeroplane and then with our experience of such operations we shall be poised ready to put it into service. At the moment, the future of VTOL is very uncertain because there is no vehicle in the world which can be operated economically on a commercial basis. I remember Sir George Edwards [chairman of the British Aircraft Corporation] saying some years ago he had little faith in VTOL. He said the amount of power you need to get the thing off the ground was such that it could never be economically produced. But that was perhaps because his company wasn't in the VTOL business.'

Sir Anthony Milward also believes in a separate existence for BEA and thinks a VTOL aircraft would ensure the short-haul airline's separate existence. He also feels that it will take 'all of 20 years' to develop a VTOL aircraft that is economic and quiet, but when it comes it will be exactly right for the airline's needs. But the development costs are in the Concorde class. At least £1,000 million is needed.

Sir Barnes Wallis, inventor of the R-100 airship, Wellington bomber, dambuster bombs and dozens of ideas incorporated in today's civil and military jets, said in January 1971 that a 3,000 mph vertical take-off plane shaped like a paper dart could be flying in ten years. The 83-years-old aviation genius, who was chief of aeronautical research for Vickers and B.A.C. for 25 years, believed it possible to produce a VTOL supersonic transport in time to save the building of a third airport for London and to avoid the spoilation of any part of our countryside.